FINANCE AND TAXES FOR THE HOME-BASED BUSINESS

by Charles and Bryane Lickson

Crisp Publications
Menlo Park

FINANCE AND TAXES FOR THE HOME-BASED BUSINESS

Charles and Bryane Lickson

Credits

Managing Editor: Kathleen Barcos
Editor: Regina Lynn Preciado
Designer: ExecuStaff
Typesetting: ExecuStaff
Cover Design: London Road Design

Copyright © 1997 by Crisp Publications, Inc.
Printed in the United States of America by Bawden Printing Company.

Distribution to the U.S. Trade:

National Book Network, Inc.
4720 Boston Way
Lanham, MD 20706
1-800-462-6420

Library of Congress Catalog Card Number 96-85514
Lickson, Charles & Bryane
Finance & Tax Planning for the Home-Based Business
ISBN 1-56052-397-2

Acknowledgments

As with any research and writing undertaking involving so complex a topic as finance and planning, the authors had considerable help. Most of the people we spoke to wished to remain anonymous and so they will. Some will be mentioned in the text. We thank the following for their significant contributions to this book: Randolph Byrd, Publisher of *Upline Magazine,* for suggesting the book; Phil Gerould, Publisher of Crisp Publications for continued faith in our writing abilities; and Andrea Zunzer, assistant to Charles at Mediate-Tech, Inc., for her support and assistance every day and especially in those final, high-pressured days as we faced deadline.

Of course, we are responsible for judgments and opinions. We stand behind these as they have been empirically shown to work; however, as with any book, we are writing in the most general terms. Many of these principles will apply to your business or practice. Some will not. It also goes without saying that no book, however well done, can substitute for the guidance and counsel of experienced professionals in the field.

Charles' dad, Len Lickson, is still active in his home-based business as a Senior Field Underwriter for New York Life (despite his chronological age past eighty). Bryane's dad, the late Dr. Carl B. Miller, a cofounder of the Council on Nutrition, spent his last years active as Secretary-Treasurer of that organization from his home office. Our mothers, Maxine Lickson and Gertrude Miller, continue to inspire us. We honor them and their contributions to our life and our love.

This book is dedicated to the newest generation in our family: Ian Matthew Stock, born in November 1995, to Charles' daughter Laura and her husband Laurence; and Sierra Eileen Goneau, born in December 1995, to Charles' daughter Karen and her husband Michael. May all their strategies in life be successful.

Feel free to use this book and its suggestions as you see fit. If you have any comments, discoveries or contributions to others that can find themselves in a new edition, please feel free to contact us at the address below:

Thanks for purchasing this book. We hope you find it not only enlightening, but also entertaining.

Charles P. Lickson
Bryane Miller Lickson
P.O. Box 607
Front Royal, VA 22630
Voice: (540) 636-2515
Fax: (540) 636-303
E-mail: MediateMTI@aol.com

Contents

CHAPTER I.
Introduction

"To be happy at home is the ultimate aim of all ambition;
the end to which every labor and enterprise tends,
and of which every desire prompts the prosecution."
—Samuel Johnson

This book is a resource for people who are engaged in home business. What is a home business? We define "home business" as considerable business or professional activities conducted by the person from the home. Following these guidelines, the test criteria for the definition is to determine the "principle headquarters" of the *activity*, not who the person is or for whom he or she works. In other words, a sales representative for a large company who is "headquartered" at home is as much a home business person as the independent computer consultant who works from his or her house.

In preparing for this book, we called upon our own experience working from home. Bryane's principal office and business are at home. As a writer, artist and consultant, Charles has an outside office where he runs a mediation, consulting and training firm, but he writes from his home office. We also called upon the experience of several other home business people, respected resources, and experts on the topic.

It probably comes as no surprise to you, the home-based business or professional person, that the number of home businesses is very large and growing rapidly.

About one million new businesses are started each year in America; of those, approximately two hundred thousand will survive five years. This translates into one in five businesses making it to their fifth anniversary. This is an alarming statistic! Why in the world would only one in five businesses in the "Land of Opportunity" survive so short a period of time? There are several reasons; however, the most common happens to be the most controllable. There is no magic equation for success, but one basic rule holds true: "A business owner who fails to plan, plans to fail." You will see as you read on that we rate planning as an *essential* element in the strategy for success of a home-based business.

If we look at percentages of the United States home-based working population, we see that of 39 million people who work at home, 31 to 32% (a little more than twelve million) self-employed individuals derive their primary income from self-employment. Presumably, the others are part-time home workers who work at home for pleasure or to supplement family income.

The National Center for Policy Analysis in Dallas says that 70% of home businesses are run by women. This figure may be changing as more men find longevity in private firms or governmental positions is no longer a sure thing. But there is no denying that in home-based business, women are number one. A big segment of home-based business is the exploding field of network marketing (sometimes also called "multilevel marketing" or "MLM). According to Randolph Byrd, publisher of *Upline Magazine*, women got to the top in MLM because "there are no glass ceilings—what you earn is what you get." In a recent issue of *Upline* dedicated to women and their successes in the filed, he went on to say: "Prejudice against women seems lovingly disarmed in network marketing." *Upline Magazine*, October 1995, page 3.

Home workers who are not proprietors of home businesses include telecommuters and employees of MLM organizations. Many individuals work from their homes but not for themselves, and many of these people are often called telecommuters. These employees communicate over the telephone and often "deliver" work via their computer or fax to the main office of the company that has hired them to work at home either part- or full-time.

The 1992 Link Resources study conducted by the Home Office/Small Business Round Table showed that there were 6.6 million United States telecommuters, which is a 20% increase from its 1991 study. Telecommuters often use their experience as an entry into establishing their own home business using contacts and skills acquired and/or sharpened while working for a mainline company.

A home worker for an MLM organization is really a distributor for network marketing whose main task is to build a "download" of more distributors into the organization. These individuals work under their recruiter and are in turn encouraged to build their own "downloads," with the process repeated again and again. If you are interested in, or are approached regarding such a tiered system, remember that certain MLM organizations are prohibited in certain states. However, some people do make good money in these ventures, so if you are interested or already involved, check the organization's legitimacy with your state or county district attorney's office and the Better Business Bureau.

People who work from home are doing well financially, according to the statistics. A June 1992 study conducted by the Home Office/Small Business Round Table on the Genie computer information service suggests that most full-time self-employed people gross $30,000 or more each year, another 10 percent gross more than $100,000 per year and some others earn as much as $250,000 per year or more in their home businesses. According to the Small Business Administration, one of every seven businesses in the United States is a home-based business.

Charting the success rate of home business is not easy to do as current data by that category has not been readily available. This is because there are no accurate statistics on failure rates applicable to this segment of the business world. Statistics for commercial businesses show that 80 to 90% of all new businesses fail in the first year and 95% fail within five years. While there can be no doubt that some home businesses do fail, the overall risks of launching a home-based business are apparently no greater than for businesses started outside the home.

Succeeding in business is tough enough without the pressures and distractions that can come from the needs of the home itself. A principal aspect of any business is its financial condition and available resources. We hope you find this book to be a valuable resource in guiding you to success.

We have tried to organize this book with you in mind and gently to guide you into some realistic personal, legal and financial issues relevant to your financial strategies. We will occasionally refer to real home business people (with their permission) and to David Reuban, a fictional composite of a number of home business people we know.

In the next chapter, we deal with some of the reality testing required of the home business person and also share some insights into planning and organizing yourself, your space and your life. Later in the book, we will journey through the planning, legal, fund-raising, asset preservation and other very pragmatic issues that must become part of your personal financial strategy.

CHAPTER II.

You and Your Home Business

"I like work; it fascinates me.
I can sit and look at it for hours."
—Jerome K. Jerome

The Industrial Revolution moved workers from their homes into factories and office buildings in towns and cities. However, many individuals, such as farmers, continued to conduct their full-time businesses at home. And others did extra work at home in addition to their new salaried or hourly wage positions.

Americans have continued this practice of the home business, influenced by national trends in popular thinking, politics, economics, inflation, population and individual needs. These individuals, regardless of background, all share an entrepreneurial spirit. Do you?

Whether you are . . .

- A caretaker or homemaker who must or chooses to be at home, or who needs or wants extra money.

- A trade worker desiring either extra or primary income as an independent contractor

- A career woman disillusioned with America's glass ceiling who decides to do for personal profit at home what she once did for someone else's ultimate benefit

- A divorced woman possessing abilities, talents and education, but finding it difficult to re-enter the job market

- An individual with disabilities or other special needs for whom better supports are available at home or who just chooses to work at home.[1]

- A manager (midlevel or higher) who has been laid off and who now supports himself and family with a home business

- A retiree desiring a second occupation to provide income and purpose to a less structured life

. . . you have decided to market your chosen specialties in your home business.

SELF-ASSESSMENT

As a home business worker you have joined a new segment of the population that began with the 1960's generation who wanted a do-it-yourself philosophy. This influencing philosophy surfaced in several aspects of daily life—from homemade clothing to home education of children to log cabin homes self-structured from kits to organized farming.

Many people see their home businesses as the hub of the wheel that connects the spokes of child raising, clean environmental living, compassionate parenting, economic cooperatives with neighbors and friends, home computer telecommuting, and home schooling. For the home business person, this lifestyle transcends the initial material incentives of most other people.

We noted in Chapter 1 the excellent earning potential of home workers. Success of many home business workers is measured not only in their percentage of annual financial growth but also in their peace of mind.

Many people who have home businesses see the business not only as a way to earn their living but also as a way of life. Now that you will be among this lifestyle group as a home business person, you will have to evaluate yourself carefully. Use the following twenty questions as a starting point.

1. Am I ready and willing to take the necessary risks to succeed?

2. Do I know how to estimate the initial start-up costs and anticipate the amount of money needed until my business makes a profit?

3. Do I have sufficient capital and resources to maintain my necessary living expenses until I am really making money?

4. Do I know what my necessary minimal living expenses are?

---

[1] Special needs are often incentives to start a home business. For information regarding adaptive devices to assist your work at home, contact your state office of rehabilitation, the IBM Special Needs Information Referral Center in Atlanta at (800) 426-3333, and/or Apple Worldwide Disability Solutions Group at (800) 732-3131.

5. If I am not successful, can I afford the financial loss? How much would it be? What repercussions could the loss have, based on financial arrangements I might undertake?

6. Why do I want to have a home business?

7. Is this the right time for me to do this?

8. Today's divorce rate is fifty percent—who owns the business?

9. Will my loved ones be supportive and understanding?

10. Will I have to relocate to access product or service needs? How will this affect my loved ones and me?

11. Do I have adequate education and skills necessary or do I need to take courses? How much will this cost in time and money?

12. Am I too young or too old to market my product or service?

13. Do I have any physical limitation or special needs to consider? If so, what are they and what effects might they have in terms of cost, time and operating procedures?

14. What special capabilities and talents do I have?

15. What personal attributes do I possess that would help promote my success? What weaknesses must I overcome?

16. Is this the right time for the product or service of my home business to be successful?

17. How do I know if there is a market for my product or service?

18. How do I plan to market my product or service

19. Is there a stigma attached to being a home-based business for my product or service? Should I downplay the fact that I work in my home rather than a traditional office building, and how do I ethically handle this?

20. Whom do I know who would be my mentor when I am uncertain about how to handle various issues? If I do not know someone already, how will I find the right person?

Truthfully answering these questions may not be easy. You may find that you don't have answers to all the questions and will have to research independently or seek aid. But the time and effort required will be worthwhile. If objectively done and your personal resolve matches with realistic considerations, you should have an itinerary of what is really ahead and a plan of how you intend to face it.

According to several successful home workers, you are more likely to succeed if you practice the following:

- Set and focus on clear goals.

- Maintain a good self-image and presentation.

- Don't procrastinate.

- Minimize interpersonal interruptions and conflicts.

- Hire or contract with the right people for each project.

- Have a master manager eye when delegating work.

- Devote an adequate amount of time—and use it well.

YOUR WORKSPACE

Once you have resolved to establish your home business, it is important to remember that unlike a commercial enterprise located in a building solely confined to industry or trade activity, the "structure" you are working within (i.e., your home) also fulfills *infinite* other requirements. Therefore, you must determine whether your workspace should be separated from nonwork activities completely, partially, or not at all.

Resolution of this question depends naturally upon the nature of your work and available space. Other considerations include your child or adult care responsibilities, financial resources, physical limitations, safety constraints and regulations, sensitivity to informal vs. formal and structured vs. unstructured atmospheres, working style, labor laws as regards cottage industry helpers, telecommunications laws and zoning laws.

CASE PROFILE

Michelle Killette is sole proprietor of Glitz, et al. Her eight-year-old extremely successful home business in McLean, Virginia, represents, in many ways, the synthesis of the attributes we have learned are necessary for not only a successful business, but also a happy life. Michelle has reached the point in her business where she could move anywhere, have many employees and a considerable growing overhead. Instead, her sister helps with jewelry design and manufacture, as do supplementary part-time workers who are called when

---

needed. And with her recent growth rate at 75% per year, they are needed more often than in the early days. As you look upon Glitz, et al's beautiful Austrian crystal jewelry creations on CBS's "As the World Turns" or in such places as Nordstrom, remember that Michelle and her helpers created the pieces in the top floor of her town home.

When evaluating your own hands-ons resources and requirements to market your home business's product or service, it may help you to determine:

- Do you have what you need?
- If not, do you need it now?
- If so, what is the estimated cost?
- If not, will you need it later?
- If so, by what date must you obtain it?
- What is the estimated cost?
- What is the total cost?

Workspace Assessment

Here are some elements to consider when deciding where and how to set up your home office. You may want to evaluate several possible locations.

- Is the space comfortable (i.e., adequate light, temperature control, furniture)?
- Is it free from distractions?
- Will you have easy access to your most frequently used work aides?
- Do you have adequate storage space for past and future projects?
- Will others quickly understand your filing system?

WORKING EFFICIENTLY FROM HOME

As an artist who is attentive to detail, Bryane has to plan accordingly because everything takes her longer as a result. Because of her own personal style she has to work hard to work smart! Perhaps you only need to work smart to accomplish your goals in half the time it might require Bryane. Does this make her work more valuable to the consumer? Probably not, but the way Bryane works requires the time. Consequently, in Bryane's home business, when pursuing her art and writing, the following checklist is helpful.

Bryane's Personal Efficiency Checklist

☐ Compile errands. Plan an organized route that results in minimal travel time and aggravation from inefficient duplication. Also compile other tasks such as returning calls, paying bills and writing notes, so total time is accounted for productively.

☐ Simplify work into parts. Determine what you want to do to prevent needless complication and detail.

☐ Think creatively.

☐ Schedule brain-charging breaks (with set time limits) to maintain and focus efficiency.

☐ Post deadline dates on a master schedule.

☐ Find the most beneficial civic activities for your interests, talents and time schedule that are compatible with your business's overall networking success.

☐ Listen to your inner voice and don't determine the worth of your ideas by the approval of others.

☐ Waste no time worrying about failure, fear or unpopularity.

☐ Structure time for constructive review and reform action and, if required, mediated interventions.

YOUR OWN BOSS

While we hope the strategies and evaluation methods suggested here will help you organize your research for creating and maintaining a successful home business, please remember that it must reflect your style and personality. Your home business must be run in a fashion that makes sense to you, even though it might drive someone else crazy!

Actually this is one of the greatest benefits of being a home businessperson. In the outside business world, corporate offices are pretty much the same. But home business offices are as different as the millions of individuals who are the office bosses.

We also know of several home businesses that really do have a separate staff and an organization. But let's face it, if there are going to be a myriad of employees and a large hierarchical structure, perhaps you belong in the high rises tower down the street and not in your lovely family room with its view.

As we look at the responsibilities and challenges of mixing the home business with home tasks there is always a blending factor. Having your business within your home necessitates that you objectively view these factors and plan accordingly. Figure 1 highlights some of the benefits and dangers of working from home.

Realizing the overlaps of positives and negatives, we offer these suggestions to prevent you from feeling overwhelmed and instead keep you positively focused on your business.

- Have your office or work space in a quiet area of your home to minimize interruptions.

- Install separate phone lines for your office phone, modem, and fax machine. Get voice mail for both your office phone and your household phone.

- Stick to a schedule. Keep personal tasks to their set scheduled time so you don't lose productive working time. Instead, combine your personal tasks and make a whole day of them, which can be a wonderful mental and physical change.

- Maintain a professional manner in all ways of interacting with the public and clients so that you are taken seriously and people will not try to infringe on your good nature. If you project yourself as a professional, others are more likely to respond promptly, well prepared, and appropriately dressed out of mutually respected of set standards.

YOUR ROLE	BENEFITS	DANGERS
Boss	You don't have to report to anyone and no one looks over your shoulder.	Requires strong self-discipline.
Scheduler	You don't have to be in and out of the office at set times or days.	Without a set schedule you might be less productive.
Solo Act	You don't waste time caught up in meetings or get side-tracked by office politics or rivalry.	You might have less mental energy due to lack of interaction, possibly to the point of loneliness or depression.
Standard Bearer	You don't have to conform to a dress code.	You might become too lax and will have to work harder to conform when meeting with other professionals.
Business Person	If your clients are late or don't show up for meetings, you aren't away from your work and thus don't lose productive working time.	Clients might take advantge of the situation. They will also see how you live.
	You don't waste time commuting.	You never really leave your work; you're always "in" your office.
	You have the flexibility to take time during the day for your personal life (errands, emergencies, phone calls, etc.).	You cannot compartmentalize your two lives as easily. You juggle your professional and personal obligations in the same environment.

FIGURE 1.

If you take good care of yourself, you protect your physical and mental health and at the same time you are your own best marketing agent. Remember one positive impression will be passed on to a minimum of ten other individuals free of charge! By the same coin, one negative impression can be very, very costly. So look your best and always do your best.

We're assuming you now agree that you're right for the home business and it's right for you. Read on and carefully ponder the necessary tasks ahead as we delve into financial strategies for you.

Chapter III.
Planning—The Strategic Prerequisite

"Doing more things faster is no substitute
for doing the right things."
—Stephen R. Covey, A. Roger Merrill
and Rebecca R. Merrill

Whatever the business or profession you plan to operate or are now operating from home, in order to succeed fully, (i.e., achieve the maximum personal and professional possibilities from the business), you should have a plan. Organized people have plans for their lives. Many of the soothsayers of modern living talk about individual and life plans for people.

A good business has a business plan. The more successful businesses even have separate plans for marketing, development and financial issues. The business plan is the overall current and long-term picture of the business. Separate plans address far more narrow but very relevant issues such as finances. Whether you undertake a general or a specific type of plan (or best yet, both forms of planning), we cannot emphasize enough the relationship of planning to success. Planning assists you in determining your needs and in designing mechanisms for satisfaction of these needs—both personal and professional.

A business plan helps entrepreneurs and business managers to think through their strategies, to balance their enthusiasm with facts and to recognize their limitations. It will help you avoid potentially disastrous errors like undercapitalizing, creating negative cash flow, hiring the wrong people, selecting the wrong location, and pursuing the wrong market.

A winning business plan requires time. We are told you should allow fifty to one hundred hours to write an effective business plan, this includes, research, documentation, analysis and review. Entrepreneurs should start planning at least six months before they initiate a new business. This takes into consideration the time you need to devote to business start-up while working another job. Six months gives you time to sharpen and focus your business ideas, test your assumptions and improve your management skills.

Nothing should happen until you convince yourself that proper business planning is an absolute necessity. Covello and Hazelgren, authors of *Your First Business Plan,* contend that your business plan is the heart and soul of your operation and probably the most important set of documents you will provide to any lending institution or potential investor. It explains all the financing you need and, most importantly, it can give potential financial sources persuasive information about your new or existing firm.

WHY DO YOU NEED A BUSINESS PLAN?

Most people think of business plans as one-purpose documents, such as for raising money. In fact, you can put your business plan to multiple uses. A comprehensive, attractively presented and realistic business plan will help you accomplish many objectives. Among such objectives, Covello and Hazelgren point out, are the following[1]:

1. Take charge of your entrepreneurial life. The business plan is evidence of your initiative. It shows that you have the discipline to focus your energies on an important project and understand how to achieve progress and growth, solve problems along the way, and achieve ultimate goals. The business plan is the foundation and pillars of your vision and will allow you to structure your ideas into reality.

2. Lay out a master blueprint. The business plan is to the entrepreneur what a set of detailed architectural drawings is to the builder. It determines the details used in reaching your objectives. It shows you the logical progression set in order to reach your established goal. It may also help you consider an alternative, and possibly better route. The business plan is a powerful management tool.

3. Communicate your master plan to members of your team. The business plan constitutes a concrete statement of purpose that allows you to communicate to your colleagues a step-by-step agenda for reaching your goals. Some portions of the business plan can also be used in training and coordinating meetings, as well as teaching staff persons what their role and accountability will be in making your business function successfully.

---

[1] Covello, Joseph and Brian Hazelgren. *Your First Business Plan.* Naperville, IL. Source Books Trade. 1993. Pages 9–10.

4. Attract money to your project. Potential suppliers of capital and other needed resources, bankers, brokers, investors, future partners, etc., will place great value on your business plan as they determine whether to participate."

Because you may never get to know the many important financial and other contracts you need on a personal basis, you should have an appropriate document to present in written form. Your business plan will be your initial selling tool (what Covello and Hazelgren call "your business resume") when attracting lenders to participate with you in your venture.

DEVELOPING YOUR OWN BUSINESS PLAN

You and your business need a mission. The goal and purpose (sometimes referred to as the "vision") of your business are the underlying philosophical structure for your business plan. Before you go any further, ask yourself if you have a clear picture of the destination for yourself, your firm and your family.

If you do, you are ready to move on to the rest of the business plan creation. If you do not yet have such a vision, it is time to return to the drawing board to create one. You can find several excellent books that discuss developing business visions, among them Peter Drucker's *Innovation and Entrepreneurship*, and Tom Peter's *The Pursuit of Wow*, or you may want to attend a seminar or workshop on the topic. In any case, we cannot stress enough the importance of knowing your business's mission before you begin to build your business plan.

You are entitled to some artistic license in creating your business plan, but sophisticated readers of your plan will soon know whether you know how to present your business's story effectively. One key test of a good business plan is its structure, a second is its overall appearance and a third factor is the credibility of the content. While business plans can take as many forms as there are businesses, most successful plans (i.e., plans used effectively to raise money or inform others about the business) have certain topic or subject matter in common.[2]

However you design and configure it, the plan should include a cover page, an executive summary, a descriptive plan and your financial data. Remember: potential investors and other important contacts will probably see your business plan before they see you. An excellent business plan helps make that first impression a good one.

---

[2] For an example of a detailed business plan outline, please see Appendix C.

The Cover Page

This should clearly identify the business and might even state briefly your reason for presenting, the plan such as i.e., "An Offer of Limited Partnership Interests." The cover should be attractive but not garish. It might have the business logo. If you have high-quality letterhead, the cover page could be presented on the letterhead.

The Executive Summary

Because this is the first and often only piece of the plan that will be looked at, the executive summary is a critical portion of an effective business plan. Investors examine this part of the plan first, yet ironically, it is usually completed after all other sections have been composed. By preparing the executive summary last, you will be able to write it more easily and with greater impact, because you have already compiled your data and are thoroughly familiar with the rest of the plan. As Covello and Hazelgren says, "Simply transfer the 'sizzle' of the plan into concise paragraphs; these become your executive summary."

Here are Covello and Hazelgren's suggestions for structuring your executive summary, along with some questions that each section should answer.

Introduction

When was your company formed?
What do you sell/distribute/manufacture/etc.?

Statement of Purpose

What product or service do you provide your customers?

Present Status

What phase of operation is your business in? If you're still in start-up mode, say so. If you are in expansion and need capital, say so. For example, if you need money to help positive cash flow, show projections that demonstrate how you will cut operating costs and increase sales by a particular percentage. These two important items will result in a faster turn of cash flow to your company.

Background

Who is the market?
What are your customers' buying habits?
How will you educate your customers about your product or service?
Who are your suppliers? Are you able to buy from different suppliers at a lower cost?

How much have you produced in annual sales over that past three to five years?

Have you operated at a loss? Why? How will you correct this problem?

What are your revenue projections for your next fiscal year? What is your projected growth rate (by percentage) for the next five years?

Concept

What is different about your product or service and how does it compare to similar ones already on the market?

Do you or your staff require special training to sell, manufacture or distribute properly your product or service?

Company Strategy

What strategies will you use to meet the competition?

If your business is already established, what market share do you presently enjoy?

If you've still starting up, what market share do you expect to enjoy?

Target Market

What is your typical customer profile? Use the market information you have gleaned from pre-planning stage.

What additional products or services might your target market respond to favorably?

Legal Protection

Are your products protected by copyright, trademark, patent laws or trade secret? (See Chapter 5 for a discussion of protecting business assets.)

Customer Survey

Have you done any market research? If so, what were the results?

Are responses from customers or potential customers favorable?

Mini-Sections

What are your business objectives?
How is the business managed?
What is your marketing strategy?
What is your financial plan?

If you are able to answer all of the above questions in a coherent, concise and readable format, you will have a solid executive summary that will stimulate interest and give powerful, persuasive information to the reader.

The Descriptive Plan

This section can be called the heart of the plan. Expanding on each area of the executive summary, it is the descriptive plan that discusses in detail what the business does now or what it expects to do with the capital being sought.

Make certain that there is additional information for every topic heading presented in the executive summary. If a topic is mentioned in the executive summary but not covered in more detail in the descriptive plan, the reader will wonder one of two things: Either the author of the plan doesn't know how to prepare a plan; or that he or she has no further substantiation for that item.

For example, suppose the executive summary states under the topic "Legal Protection": "The company expects to seek maximum legal protection for its products under the laws of the United States." Within the descriptive plan, the topic "Legal Protection" might say: "The company has created novel products that it expects to protect wherever possible. Patent and copyright counsel have been (or will be) retained to review applicability of patent, trademark, copyright and other intellectual property legal protection available to the company. A portion of the funds raised pursuant to this plan will be used to afford adequate legal protection for company products." This is how the descriptive plan expands upon the executive summary.

Each portion of the descriptive plan is important. The financing source will look at three key things about your business: (1) The quality or innovation of your product or service, (2) the potential market for the product or service, and (3) the adequacy or qualification of management to make the business succeed. The best product ideas can fail if management doesn't know how to get the job or service done. On the other hand if you have wonderful managers but an uninteresting product you will fall flat on your face. It is also true that you can have a wonderful product and a great management team, but if you don't know how to sell the item, failure is inevitable.

To satisfy the reader of the plan that you are credible and can meet the three criteria above your description of the service or product you are offering becomes critical. Let the reader see the market potential and understand the justification for the infusion of capital into such a good idea. So, critical to the descriptive plan is a section called, "The Product" or "The Services Offered by the company." Remember, the reader will always be looking for ways in which your product or service is different or better than existing products or services.

Next in the descriptive plan should be a discussion of management. Those people (including you) who will administer the funds raised and manage the firm must be identified with statements of their qualifications including education and past experience. As noted above, the reader of the plan must see that the product or service is exciting and the team to bring it forth is fully qualified. As noted elsewhere, you may want to include full biographies or resumes or key players. If you do, summarize the background of each in the management section of the descriptive plan and attach the resumes as appendices.

Once you show that the product or service is interesting, and the management team is the appropriate choice, than you must show how you plan to bring it all to market. The "Sales and Marketing" section of the business plan discusses that. If you have a marketing plan, you will want to summarize it here. If the whole plan is not too lengthy, attach it as an appendix. Discuss ways in which your team will move your wonderful product or service from inside your home into someone else's home or business. In other words, talk about how you are going to sell what you have to offer.[3]

If you are going to hire an advertising agency or independent marketing source, be sure to name that company and include a statement of its experience and past successes in your filed. If a portion of the funding you seek will be used for marketing, note that with a cross reference to "Allocation" or "Use of Funds."

Any investor or lender will want to know how the funds sought are to be used. A part of the descriptive plan should discuss "Use of Funds." Here, be as accurate as you can, keeping in mind that there are always unexpected expenses. If you have designated specific amounts to specific items, be sure to specify these. The example below is a fairly standard business plan format for this section.

"The company expects to receive $150,000 if all shares offered are sold (or if the full loan request is granted). It is expected that the funds will be allocated as follows:

Administrative expenses (including clerical support)	$ 25,000
Equipment purchases (including new computer)	$ 10,000
Advertising and Marketing	$ 65,000
Working Capital	$ 50,000
	$150,000

If less than the full amount sought is received, the company will apply such funds to items listed above on a pro rata basis. Any funds not immediately needed for operations will be placed in fully secure income-bearing accounts."

Details of how the funds will be spent will be included in the financial data which is discussed next.

Your Financial Data

The Small Business Administration and most lenders or investors will want to have the following financial data, *as a minimum*, in the plan:

1. Balance sheet (or current financial statement of the firm). Make sure to note both long-term and current assets and liabilities as well as potential collateral.

---

[3] Crisp Publications has a number of excellent titles in the area of marketing and telemarketing that may be helpful.

2. Personal financial statement of the principal(s).

3. Projected revenues (and costs) for one to five years.

4. List of current or anticipated contractual obligations such as real estate or equipment leases.

In addition to the foregoing, don't be surprised if your personal credit report is requested. Some plans also include detailed cash flow projections with cumulative negative-positive monthly cash flow data noted. A number of spreadsheet and business plan software products can make this part much easier.

A welcome addition to the plan is a statement from an outside, disinterested party, usually an accountant, as to the efficacy of the financial projections and other assumptions.

FOCUS ON FINANCIAL PLANNING

As you plan for the financial issues and eventual success of your home business, you will note that both financial policy and financial control are key elements. As respected financial author and consultant David Bangs says, "Policy and control are the key ingredients of any successful business. Policy establishes what your business will do. Control measures the accomplishment of policy goals."[4]

In considering proper set-up of the financial side of your business, please keep in mind the significance of the accounting system. Before you start the business, if possible, try to get an experienced business accountant to set up a system that will give you adequate accounting records. This will cost some money, but as your business grows, you will find that it was well worth it.

If you feel you can't afford to have an outside professional accountant assist in setting up the system, you should ask yourself whether you are adequately funded. In fact, Bangs says, "If you don't understand the need for accounting records, you don't have enough management experience to be starting a business." That may be a little harsh for us, but we do want to alert you that many small businesses underestimate the importance of setting up a proper accounting system. Often, they will try to catch up when they have more money. It may be too late then and records, controls and growth suffer.

The system will reflect the policy of your business, but that is only half the battle. The other half is control. It doesn't take a genius to figure out that if you don't control your business, it will control you. James Gill notes that control works in two ways. First, "it helps you do better what you are now doing," and second, "it helps you prepare for expansion or change."[5] We'll look at both of these aspects.

---

[4] Bangs, David. *The Business Planning Guide.* Dover, NH, Upstart Publishing Company. 1992. Page 53.

[5] Gill, James. *Financial Basics of Small Business Success.* Crisp Publications. 1994.

Business Policy

Would you agree that the overriding policy of your business is to find out what your markets want (marketing), to satisfy those wants (production or delivery), and to make a profit while doing so (proper execution)? If you agree with these underlying policy goals, doesn't it make sense implementing your policy depends on planning and using your plan as a means of controlling your business outcome?

The Control Document

Bangs suggests five documents that will help you maintain control:

- Income statement
- Cash flow analysis
- Break-even analysis
- Balance sheet
- Deviation analysis

Two essential financial statements, the **income statement** and the **cash flow projection** reflect the good manager's objectives. The income statement (also called the profit and loss or P.&L. statement) shows how well the business is doing over a defined period of time by subtracting expenses from sales. The cash flow projection shows how well the business is managing its cash (liquidity) by subtracting disbursements (actual cash outlays or outflow) from cash received (income or inflow).

Maintaining the balance between profitability and liquidity (sufficient cash, or assets quickly convertible to cash) is one of the great financial challenges of any business. Rapid growth (with high profits) can deplete cash, causing illiquidity. Ironically, a number of businesses have been known to fail even while they are profitable. We're sure you can think of a business that appeared to be doing very well but over-expanded, over-hired or over-produced too quickly and ran out cash and failed.

Projected income and **cash flow statements** should help you spot these kinds of severe problems and vulnerabilities in time to do something to fix them. You may have to raise new capital or arrange for the right kind of financing. The next chapter discusses in detail several options that may be available to you.

The **break-even statement** is based on the income and cash flow statements. Break-even analysis is a technique that every business should have because it shows the volume of revenue from sales you need to balance exactly the sum of your fixed and variable expenses. You can also use this document to make decisions in such critically important areas as setting prices, whether and when to purchase or lease equipment, projecting profits or losses at different revenue or sales volumes, and whether or not to expand your staff.

The **balance sheet** records the past effect of all the financial decisions taken in the business. It also records the cash position (liquidity) of the business and what the owner's equity is at a given point in time. These are directly affected by the cash flow and income statements, which record how the business operates over time.

The **deviation analysis** compares actual performance to projected or budgeted performance on a monthly basis. You can think of the deviation analysis as an alarm ready to warn you when the business is operating too far afield from the plan. This document or report allows you to compare both income statement and cash flow projections against actual performance. It is a known fact that small errors (the hidden ones) sink more businesses than larger (easily recognizable) errors. The deviation analysis can help you catch them in time.

These five report and control documents provide, when used together, a comprehensive model of the operations, liquidity, and the past and near future of your business.

ESTABLISHING A BOOKKEEPING SYSTEM

A logical first step toward managing your business for profit is to establish a bookkeeping system that can provide you with the raw data you will need for the five control documents discussed above. The bookkeeping system should be simple enough for you or an employee to update daily and it should provide for weekly, monthly, quarterly and yearly summaries. It must contain day-to-day cash controls. A checkbook and a cash register tape or a computerized report such as from Quicken™ will be part of the basics of your bookkeeping system. Beyond this, you should tailor your own home business's method of bookkeeping to your specific needs.

Your business's bookkeeping system is the basis of your business information (control) system. You know best what kind of information you will require beyond the suggestions we have made here. We have not presumed in this book to set up a system for you. For one, we are not qualified. We have a financial person in-house whose responsibility is both system set-up and execution. She reports twice weekly on payables, receivables and general status. She also handles tax issues, payroll and long-term financial planning.

For your own business, you have three resources for setting up your bookkeeping system: an in-house bookkeeper who could be you, business service firms and accountants. Each has advantages and drawbacks. You should decide which suits your needs best.

Manual or software-based do-it-yourself systems are lowest in cost but require more time and often provide less information than professional business service firms or accountants. We acknowledge that business service firms and accountants cost considerably more but they can save you time and a lot of headaches. We suggest you carefully consider all three before making your decision. Keep in mind that business service firms and accountants serve in an adjunct or outside capacity for your business and as a part of their services can make some helpful suggestions that go beyond their pure accounting or financial mission. It could very well be that a cost-saving suggestion or customer contact generated by one of the outside services justifies the higher costs.

A good accountant (whether with a business service or a CPA firm) can provide analysis and interpretation of your financial statements, wide experience with other small businesses including those special needs of home business people, knowledge about local people and markets, advice on choosing and applying the considerable computer power now available for financial needs, and other general managerial insights.

Of course, for tax issues and questions, we strongly suggest an outside professional. You do not want to worry about taxes you might owe or payments for taxes for employees or sales or other obligations to state, federal or local governments. It has been said (probably originally by accountants) that a good tax accountant can actually make you more money in tax savings than he or she costs in fees.

The five control documents discussed provide the structure for your planning efforts. As Bangs says, "Properly used, they can also act as a budgeting tool, an early warning system, a problem intensify, and a solution generator." He also points out that having these tools alone is not enough. You must use them well. If used inconsistently or not at all, they are worthless. And as he reminds us, "Used incorrectly they are dangerous. Misleading financial information can lead to making bad or disastrous decisions."

Financial documents scare many people. In many ways, these documents get a bad rap because they are often complex and complicated. But they don't have to be that way. As you work on them yourself or in consultation with an outside professional, be sure to develop your financial statements with an eye on your own business and personal information needs, using common sense and your accountant's experience as guides to the level of detail needed.

It is essential to use the statements systematically. Make it policy to spend some dedicated time (preferably free from distractions) each month checking them over, once your business is generating expenses and revenue. By keeping as current as you can and using the most recent data available, you will be able to plan profitable strategies, make good business decisions, and set reasonable objectives for both yourself and the business.

Computer-based programs such as spreadsheets, accounting software, financial planning software and others will create opportunities for "what if" projections. If you are not familiar with computerized financial models, check with a good computer store or an independent software consultant familiar with accounting software. You can also consult the nearest business school (or your accountant). Being able to trace out the short-term financial implications of a business decision by using a computer model can make a big difference in the quality of your judgments, which should result in dramatic increases in profits.

We wouldn't dare to choose which of the control documents is most important, but we'll pass along David Bang's opinion: "If there is only a single statement that is available, let it be your cash flow. A business that can't pay its bills can't stay in business for long even though the business may be operating at a profit."

The ideal accounting system should be a working model of your business. A good manager has two concurrent objectives (which may seem sometimes to be inconsistent with each other): to make a profit, and to pay bills as they come due. You will note in the next chapter that we define bankruptcy as inability to meet current obligations as they become due. This is something you want to avoid!

As with so many topics in this book, there are several very good resources both in book and software form which can be helpful to you when creating your business plan and bookkeeping system. A number of these are listed in the Resources section of this book.

CONSIDERING FINANCIAL NEEDS

We have mentioned the need to take measures to assure that your business has adequate capital to meet its financial needs. Later chapters discuss and emphasize the importance of adequate capital.

One rule of thumb is relevant here: With a new business, "adequate" capital really means "more" capital than you think you need. For most new businesses, you should have sufficient capital on hand to finance the business's overhead expenses (with little or no income) for at least one year. This point is appropriately modified by those businesses or practices that will generate income immediately, such as auto mechanic, physician, appliance repair and architect.

It goes without saying that financial needs are an essential element in launching or successfully continuing a home-based business. The following will assist in delineating your financial needs and coalescing those needs into a coherent business plan.

The financial needs of the personally owned home business or practice fall into four distinct phases: (1) planning and start-up costs (prior to business launch), (2) initial operating costs, (3) continuous or regular operating costs, (4) retirement planning/life transition needs.

We'll say a few words about each category then ask you to take some time to think about how each of these categories applies to you. If you need help in coming up with items for consideration in each category, feel free to refer to the lists in Appendix A or to consider some of the lists later in this chapter.

Planning and Start-Up Costs

These include such expenses as market research, surveys, purchase of samples for evaluation, business licenses, and legal and accounting planning costs.

Initial Operating Costs

These include one-time start-up costs such as equipment purchase or lease deposits for equipment, deposits for telephone and other utilities, software purchase and usage charges, expenses to form and organize the business (including legal expenses if any), initial supplies and printing of stationery, brochures and other marketing and imaging-building materials. Many of these costs fall into the capital outlay area (see Chapter 6 for details of the account areas).

Continuous or Regular Operating Costs

Unlike the capital or start-up expense items, these cost items are the regular overhead and operating expenses you can anticipate every month. One might call these the general and administrating or the operating overhead. They include such things as rent (if you have any—your home location can save you money here, and the business might even pay rent to you if your tax planner says there is value to you in that), phone, fax, computer online time, insurance, wages, taxes, and hospitalization or other fringe benefits offered, if any. Some of these overhead expenses can be allocated between home and business. Watch this one because the IRS has gotten very tough recently on the tax ramifications of home businesses. But despite all the rigorous IRS rules that are being evaluated for additional changes as this book is going to press, if your principal place of business is in the home *and you can prove it*, there will be considerable tax advantages to you on the expense side. Again, you should consult your tax planner.

Retirement Planning/Life Transition Needs

These are those important expenses that will affect your quality of life in later years and the future of the business. By business or life transition, we mean those things that relate to what will happen to you and/or the business in later years. Will you sell? Will an heir inherit the business? Will you merge? How active will you be and for how long?

Each of the factors listed above and others you might think of should be part of the long-term planning for the business and for yourself. After all, we know that there is more than just you involved. Issues about how to structure the business for the long term are dealt with in Chapter 4 (Legal and Tax Considerations) and Chapter 6 (Funding Considerations). Actual expenses under this category might include a retirement plan (IRA, Keogh or 401(k) or pension or profit-sharing plan). They can include hospitalization and major medical, long-term disability, key person life insurance and other expenses designed to protect both you and the business when you are no longer interested in it or able to be your best. As you plan for your future, it is not too early to consider estate planning and how your business factors into your will. Furthermore, you do not want catastrophic medical expenses to undo all the good work you will have done in creating your successful home business.[6] Chapter 8 discusses long-term planning in more detail.

PLANNING FOR EXPANSION OR BUSINESS GROWTH

You are taking a huge risk when you start to expand a business, but you can minimize that risk if you plan. It makes no difference whether you are starting from scratch, buying an existing business or expanding your current business. You need to have a realistic plan based on careful research, investigation and analysis. You data must include market research, a business and marketing plan and a financial plan.

The financial plan is based on market potential, your pricing strategy, sales forecast and knowledge of the facilities and equipment you will need to buy. This statement will help you predict your fixed and variable expenses for your type of business and aid you in obtaining start-up money. If your data are accurate and objective, your financial plan will project your financial needs, break-even point and profits for the next several months, first year and two additional years. This plan should be updated monthly and annually throughout your business life.

Most business plans contain projected revenue/income (and expense) figures called pro forma reports. Pro forma means a forecast, and, based on good data, the pro forma income statement can help convince banks to loan you money or attract investors. The pro forma statement looks just like the income statement you use or will use in your business. It consists of:

Sales or Service Revenue. Cash and credit sales—your total revenue from the business. Do not include any revenue not made from the business. Other revenue, such as interest from a savings account, certificate of deposit or other income must be handled or reported in a different account. The reason for this caveat is if you include the money, even interest on money already made by the business in past years, you won't have a true picture of your operating income, which will distort your decisions. If you are thinking of buying an existing business, watch out for this sort of distortion that others may have created.

Cost of Sales. Cost of the merchandise if you retail it or sell by mail, etc.

Gross Margin of Profit. The difference between sales dollars and cost of sales dollars. From this figure you will pay salaries, rent, advertising and other expenses.

---

[6] Bryane's book on living wills and durable powers of attorney for health care documents can help you plan the same kind of dignity and respect in the end of your life as you would expect and plan for during the height of your business career. It also suggests ways to protect your estate from financial devastation in the event of the recommendation for medical life support. Bryane Miller (Lickson), *Dignified Departure,* San Jose, CA. R & E Publishers. 1995.

Expenses.   This category includes such items as:

- Advertising
- Consumable supplies (used in the business—that is, not for sale)
- Depreciation
- Employee/Owner life insurance
- Health insurance
- Interest
- Leased equipment
- Miscellaneous
- Net profit before federal taxes
- Owner's draw (if any)
- Professional expenses
- Rent
- Repairs and maintenance
- Salaries
- Social security taxes
- Taxes
- Telephone
- Transportation
- Unemployment insurance
- Utilities
- Vacation/Sick pay

The general rule is that if you are thinking of going into business, you should prepare pro forma statements, both income and cash flow, before investing time, money and energy.

Most people think of business growth or expansion as a good thing for a business—and it is. But expansion can come unexpectedly and quickly and be very disconcerting, if not fatal, to the business, so you better be ready for it. Ideally expansion will come more slowly, arriving in a properly planned-for way. Gill alerts us that this growth can come

in many forms such as increased sales, increased profits, increased fixed assets, increased expenses, increased staffing, increased borrowing—

increased everything except cash or money on hand. Unexpected and quick growth is not bad, if it can be handled. Expansion is expensive, so there is no use in making it so expensive that you can't afford it if you don't have to.

One of the reasons businesses fail when they suddenly and unexpectedly expand is that their principals assumed they could handle the increases without planning and careful attention to expansion needs. It is ironic but true that over-confident management could be the reason for the demise of an otherwise healthy venture. All too many companies look like they will go on forever, but instead end up in failure and disarray.

Gill points out that understanding the value of planning for growth can come too late.

Business scrap heaps are littered with skeletons of one-person businesses that grew more than 2,000% in four to six years. The owners thought it would go on forever and fueled the growth with ever-increasing spending. Then one day the company stopped growing, and the cut-backs began. What was once a great place to work became an increasing hostile environment.

As tough as it may be to do, you may sometimes need to slow your company's growth. This may be especially true in the home business environment, where you went to escape some of the very things that too-rapid expansion might bring. Perhaps the ideal is slow growth while absorbing the increasing volume of business. For productive go-getters, slowing growth is often a more difficult task than getting the initial business. Difficult as it may be, slowing growth will allow time to prepare for more growth in the future.

A thoroughly considered, comprehensive growth strategy is important not only to the start-up company but also to the more experienced firm. For the more successful firm with some history, as Gill notes, "The question is no longer whom can I sell to, since customers are now coming to you, but how I can have the latest technology to satisfy the increasing volume of business and my customers' needs and wants."

Thus, you will see that your clients or customers truly remain the focus of your expansion plans just as they did in the initial phase of the firm. A successful business strategy for expansion means that the strategic planning should prepare for sustained expansion: to control that growth and to integrate it into a standard way of doing business. This includes preparing to support the additional resources needed to carry out this growth in a reasonable and *sustainable* way. After all, rapid growth is not a measure of business success if it doesn't include profitability or productivity and continued or sustained levels of expanded business.

Since expanded sales and increasing revenues are so captivating, they can tempt business owners to forget that obtaining more sales, receivables and inventory without increasing support from more people, equipment and other needs invites disaster. As noted above, these disasters usually come from owners' over-confidence and their desire to outstrip quickly the competition and prove how good they are.

Do you want to show everybody how quickly you can grow or do you want to build a solid business with slow, sustainable growth?

We've talked so far about avoiding trouble (with the valuable assistance of Gill), but that is just one reason to plan growth. Of even greater importance to the business is the long-term strategic value of controlling growth. Business growth is one of a number of the business variables which deserve control in the business equation. As Gill notes, no growth, slow growth, or less growth may be just what is called for at a particular time. That's when it really gets tough because "you must be willing to forgo selling opportunities, limit your market share and keep money in the bank rather than spend it. Planned growth means that balance can be maintained, and that even rapid growth can be accommodated and does not have to ruin the company. Growth at any price can mean that the price is too high."

We certainly acknowledge that you probably will want to expand the market for your goods or services. It is generally accepted that the three basic ways to do that are:

1. Market penetration, which means selling more of your current products or supplying additional services to your established clients or customers.

2. Market extension, which means luring new customers or clients away from the competition.

3. New product or service introduction, which means persuading customers to buy something new or use a new service offering.

ON YOUR OWN

Expansion can change everything. It obviously has positive benefits, but it can also have destructive or harmful attributes. This test (which you may find requires considerable thought) should give you some valuable insight as to your own personal relationship with expansion and success.[7]

Do you see your business expanding while preserving the original goals and mission and lifestyle commitments you made to yourself and others? Or will they change and, if so, how will that change manifest itself?

1. Economic expansion (i.e., business growth):

   a. Where will my business expand?

   _____

   _____

   b. How will my business grow?

   _____

   _____

   c. When will it grow?

   _____

   _____

   d. What will the business expansion need?

      i. Financially:

      _____

      _____

      ii. Personally:

      _____

      _____

---

[7] For more insights and self-tests for improving your own relationship to yourself and your work, please see Jeff Lickson's book *The Continuously Improving Self,* Crisp Publications, 1992.

2. Expanded goals:

   a. My original goals (for my business):

   _____

   _____

   For myself:

   _____

   _____

   b. My expanded goals (for my business):

   _____

   _____

   For myself:

   _____

   _____

   c. How does expansion add or detract from these goals?

   _____

   _____

CHAPTER IV.

Legal and Tax Implications of Home Business Structure

"The law can make you quit drinking; but it can't make you quit being the kind that needs a law to make you quit drinking."

—Don Marquis

Decisions about the financial strategies for your home-based business are not minor. In fact, many of the same factors that pertain to large, multifacility organizations also apply to your own decisions.

The legal structure and ownership of your business are very relevant to these types of decisions. While this book is not a legal guide, it is impossible to have a realistic discussion about business finance without some basic presumptions about legal organizational form. It is an unfair, unrealistic and incorrect presumption that a home-based business is usually a sole proprietorship. While it is true that many service, craft or artistic businesses that have a home base are sole proprietorships (especially where it is essentially a one-person operation), home based business reflects as wide a range of legal structures as non-home-based business.

To demonstrate more clearly the relationship between your business's legal structure and financial strategies, this chapter begins with a quick and simplistic summary of business organization law.[1]

If you are willing to risk formation of the legal organization without an attorney, you can consult a professional corporate formation company (e.g., U.S. Corporation Company and CorpAmerica Inc., both of whom will form a

---

[1] The source for this material is *Legal Guide for Small Business* by Charles P. Lickson from Crisp Publications. We will hereafter refer to this book as the *Legal Guide*. There are a number of other valuable resources that give you more detail about the pluses and minuses of particular legal structures. Several of these other books are listed in the Resources section later in this book. Information is also available from the Small Business Administration, your reference librarian, and even, as you will see later, on the Internet.

company for you just about anywhere in the United States) or even try your luck at filling in the blanks of a legal software program (such as "PC Attorney"™ or "Legal Expert"™).

Of course, we do not advise you to undertake such an important task as designing your legal structure without consulting both your attorney and accountant. But the truth is, many people develop the structure on their own—with readability available, off-the-shelf guides.

Critical to your decision about structure must be your business goals and the financial decisions that support them. What follows next are some of your financing decision considerations.

Because this is a book about financial issues and considerations, it will not say much about the kind of planning and thinking needed to launch a home business or practice. We assume that your business or practice is already under way or in the serious planning stage. You should already have given the proposed home business or practice concentrated thought, planning and consideration of the many factors which must go into the decision to move your business home or to start a business of your own.[2]

As you prepare to review your financial needs and considerations, ask yourself: what form should my home business or practice take? To answer this perfectly appropriate question, you must first determine what your home business will do. If it is to be a **service-oriented business** (such as appliance repair), it may very well be that a **sole proprietorship** is the best form for you. If you and an associate are offering **professional** or **advisory services**, a **partnership** may fit your needs. Where products are concerned and considerable contact is expected with the public, a **corporation** is probably best for you.

Most people who are considering how to structure their home business or practice should take an interest in the practical convenience, personal liability, potential for financial reward, and tax implications of each option. Since what the home business or practice does is so critical to the proposed form, before you can ask what legal form shall my business take, you must first consider what your home business or practice do. Some guidelines for business forms that relate to what the business does are the following (of course these are generalizations and may not apply to your situation):

- If you engage in a service business that does not open your premises to the general public, (e.g., accounting, business advisory, consulting, writing, public relations) you may be best off with a sole proprietorship.

- If your home business or practice has a service component and requires or envisions a special relationship with someone besides you, (e.g., another

---

[2] A helpful resource on business planning and launch is Professor Charles Martin's book *Your New Business: A Personal Plan for Success*, available from Crisp Publications.

accountant, physician, consultant) and also does not invite the general public upon the premises, a partnership may be the best arrangement for you.

- If you plan to offer a product for sale or expect to invite members of the public into the business premises, a corporation might be best. This would also be true if you were going to raise funds and needed shares to sell.

- If you share a very specific project with another person or firm but wish to maintain your own independence, a joint venture may be perfect for you.

In addition to asking yourself what the home business or practice will do, you should also think about how much money your home business or practice will need and where will the money come from. The methodology of financing a business is closely connected with the form of organization chosen. One cannot sell shares in a sole proprietorship. On the other hand, if a loan or gift is being made to supply the start-up capital, sole proprietorship can work just fine.

This book is about financial considerations in the general sense and not specifically about raising venture capital, so we will not dwell on the challenges posed by raising capital (although we offer some suggestions in Chapter 6). We will state unequivocally that the business should not be launched until its financing plan is carefully thought out and provided for. The form of the organization can assist in providing for adequate capitalization. Unfortunately, the corollary is also true: if the business organization form is incorrect, it can inhibit if not eliminate your ability to adequately capitalize the business.

For example, if the business needs to raise considerable funds on the strength of the business concept (and not necessarily the person running or owning it), a corporation would probably be the best form because it affords a mechanism (sale of shares) to raise funds. On the other hand, if two people are going into their own service business and each agrees to contribute an agreed amount of the start-up capital, partnership sounds like the ideal form. An accountant or financial advisor can make a real contribution when it comes to the financial relevance of the form of business organization.

In addition to the foregoing considerations, a major personal planning question to ask before you decide on a legal form of organization is: what are my personal long-term goals? If you are forming the home business or practice to provide a living and a current source of revenue, or for personal satisfaction in the present, perhaps sole proprietorship is the form of choice.

If you are not so concerned about what happens to the business after your death but are more concerned with current capability, partnership may be most suitable. However, if you are starting a business that has a life of its own which will last even beyond your own lifetime, you probably want to form a corporation.

As you have seen, when considering a legal organization for your home business or practice, you must think about what happens in the present and *what will happen to the business in the future?*

FUNDAMENTAL CONSIDERATIONS
FOR THE HOME BUSINESS FORM

You should not make a choice on the form of the organization without being clear about all four of these factors:

- What the home business or practice will do.

- How the home business or practice will be financed.

- What are your personal long-term goals?

- Will the home business have employees?

Perhaps a working example can help about now. Let's check into David Reuban's situation (Remember that David Reuban is a fictional character based on a compilation of individuals, businesses, and situations we have known.)

CASE PROFILE

Approximately one year ago, David Reuban learned that his future with his firm was bleak. This was disappointing, disheartening, and even frightening for David, as he had one child in college, another soon to go, and no personal wealth to fall back on. David and his wife Phyllis lived in a comfortable middle-to-upper-class neighborhood in suburban Washington, D.C.

David assumed his future had been secure with the rapidly growing telecommunications firm with which he had spent over then years. He began as a salesman calling mostly on government accounts. His talent, selling ability, and management skills were recognized by his boss, Jerry, president and founder of the firm. Two years ago, when Jerry asked David if he would leave selling to manage a new research and development team, David requested time to think about it.

In fact, David was doing well financially at a small salary plus commission; but he did not like the insecurity of commission sales. He also thought this new management position would allow him to use some valuable skills he had learned while getting his MBA at night. The position offered a decent, reliable salary. David accepted.

Under David's supervision, the team began to develop a sophisticated encryption coding and decoding system for sale to the military and intelligence communities.

When the bottom fell out of the federal budget and even existing programs fell to the political axe, Jerry knew that his company now had a sophisticated and expensive product (which had taken a full year and many dollars to finance) that he could not sell. Jerry knew he had to make his

---

own cuts or his firm would go the way of so many firms that relied on the government market. Reluctantly, he laid off David and the whole research and development team. He offered David two months' salary as severance pay. When David was cut loose from his employer of ten years he was in a near panic. He tried to stay calm and he was reassured by his own talent, background, and optimism he would find a new position. The truth was, he was forty-nine years old, in a highly competitive job market, and starting his search just at a time when reductions in staff size—not new hiring—were the order of the day in both the private and public sectors.

He and his wife discussed the situation and decided that because they could financially survive for awhile without David's salary and their comfortable home had a lovely finished basement, it was time to venture into a home business. The natural business for David was to consult in management along the lines of his recent in-house experience. Thus, David Reuban Associates was born.

Now that the decision was made to form David Reuban Associates, the next question was: How to organize the new business?

Although no rental space was needed, David realized he did need several thousand dollars in equipment and supplies. Also there would be other expenses such as a phone and promotional materials. Although David's dad offered to assist in financing the venture and several of David's colleagues also wanted to invest and participate, David and Phyllis preferred to retain complete independence and control over the business. They decided to finance the business themselves with a ten thousand dollar bank loan.

Phyllis asked her brother Bill, a lawyer, for advice on what form of legal organization the new firm should take. Bill asked David, first, what the business would do. David explained that it would be an individualized management consulting service. Bill asked whether any product was involved and whether people would frequently visit David's "office." David answered "no" to both.

Next, Bill asked about financial needs and David told him that he and Phyllis had already taken out a personal loan to finance their anticipated start-up expenses.

Finally, Bill asked about David's personal goals in the business. David responded that his management abilities were not being appreciated by any potential employer and that he needed creative job satisfaction. He also said he expected to earn enough money to supplement Phyllis's part-time salary. Bill then asked David about his growth plans for the business, to which David replied that he would be satisfied with a small, successful business that would occupy him much of the time and support the family's lifestyle, but it did not need to be full-time.

After considering David's plans, motivation and goals, Bill suggested a sole proprietorship with David registering to do business under a protected trade name in his community.

As you can see, a simple legal structure and form suited David and Phyllis at this stage. To assist you in a sense of real-life possibilities for a home business and the financial implications that flow from it, we will follow the development of David Reuban Associates during its growth and legal maturity.

OTHER FINANCIAL FACTORS IN START-UP STRUCTURE

While questions about home business or practice purpose, financial needs, and personal goals are essential to considering the best form of the business, you must also weigh a number of other factors. We do not deal with these in detail here, but we discuss them now to alert you to consider them regarding your chosen legal form of organization.

What licenses (from official agencies) or permissions (from private or public sources) will you need to obtain before undertaking the proposed home business or practice activity (e.g., a health department certificate to operate a restaurant)?

Are there restrictions on the proposed name (because of prior use by others or potential for consumer confusion)?

Check into special regulatory or physical requirements to carry out the home business or practice (such as locating in a properly zoned place or obtaining a variance).

Think about real estate considerations such as location, traffic rules, parking needs and access for the disabled.

Further information on these legal forms of organizations and their positive and negative attributes follows. You must consider what activity your home business or practice will engage in as you read. Remember that by putting off a decision about form, you may have made a choice you did not expect. **If you start your home business or practice without taking any action to form a particular organization, the law will impose upon it the form best fitting its structure and activity** *whether you like it or not*. In most cases, if it involves an individual in business, that form would be a sole proprietorship. Where two or more parties engage in a home business or practice enterprise without an agreement or evidence to the contrary, the law will presume a partnership was meant.

As you think about the correct form for your home business, be certain to weigh carefully each of the business structures discussed below from a number of different frameworks, including:

- Legal implications and obligations.
- Costs and time frame for organizing.
- How many people will be involved in the home business or practice.
- Your financial needs and how to best satisfy them.
- Access to professional advice and counsel.

- Tax implications and reporting requirements.
- Need for continuity.
- Whether good will should have independent value.

Sole Proprietorship

This is clearly the easiest type of home business or practice organization to form and the structure (or lack of it) which gives you the most freedom. We have used the term "sole proprietorship" to indicate and remind you that if anyone else is involved (other than as an employee, consultant or creditor), your business may be treated as a partnership. Some commentators have referred to this structure as "proprietorship." In our view, the terms are synonymous.

How To Form a Sole Proprietorship

Simply start to do business. As noted above, you will be presumed to be doing business in the form of sole proprietor. You don't need formal documents, filing or special regulatory compliance to operate as a sole proprietor. The name of the business may have to be filed or protected and cannot interfere with someone else's business or confuse the public, but legal requirements are minimal.

A sample certificate of doing business as a sole proprietor is included in Appendix B.

The Good News and the Bad News of Sole Proprietorships

The good news is that sole proprietors have the benefit of freedom from control by other associates and thus retain full independence of action. They also need to comply with minimal regulatory and governmental rules—i.e., formation of this model is automatic without any special need for attorneys or other advisers to help create it.

The bad news is that sole proprietors have unlimited *personal* liability because there is virtually no difference between their business and themselves. This liability applies to business-related incidents (such as an accident on the premises) and debts arising from the home business or practice (such as purchase of supplies).

With this proprietorship choice you may also find some challenges to raising capital. Because the home business or practice is wholly owned by the sole proprietor there is no mechanism to receive investment. Of course, loans to the proprietor are possible (assuming you can find a cooperative bank).

Employee Issues of Sole Proprietorships

As you will learn from any discussion about the legal obligation of employers to employees and worker to worker, an employer has certain minimal obligations to anyone who works for him or her. This is true notwithstanding the legal form or structure of the home business or practice. Thus, if you should choose a sole proprietorship, be prepared to obtain workers' compensation insurance and to contribute to state-sponsored programs such as unemployment insurance. Of course, you will have to comply with all the other requirements of law that apply to any employer.

Tax Implications of Sole Proprietorships

What may be perceived as an additional benefit of this form of organization is the tax treatment of sole proprietorships. Since there is no legal (or tax law) distinction between a proprietorship and the individual owner, all income is reported as part of his or her regular Form 1040 tax return. Schedule "C" is used for this purpose. As you can see, this means that revenues from the home business or practice are includable in ordinary income and that expenses (or losses) from the home business or practice are deductible.

A good friend of ours, who happens to be a former vice president of a major national bank and a sophisticated investor and who owns many rental properties and a major convenience store franchise, operates as a sole proprietor because of the tax advantage he perceives in this form. He does this despite the potential personal liability from dealing with the general public. He considers that risk as insurable. To him the ability to total all the revenues, deduct the operating expenses then apply losses or gains to other income is an attractive benefit of this form of organization.

If tax considerations factor into your choice of the home business or practice form, a sole proprietorship may be just right for you. Be sure to check with your tax adviser before making this choice for tax purposes alone.

UPDATE ON DAVID'S CASE

In David's case, the sole proprietor form was perfect in the beginning. After all, the consulting business was his own business (with the moral and financial support of his wife Phyllis). After a rocky start as David sought out clients, things began to go well. A major telecommunications firm (a competitor of David's old firm) asked David to develop a new product for it. David was torn. On the one hand, this represented his first potentially profitable account. On the other hand, he knew he needed help in doing the work. He had to choose whether to take on this big job and grow or pass on the job and stay independent.

Phyllis advised going for the job and David accepted the assignment. David soon contacted Mary, a former colleague, and asked if Mary could moonlight. Mary felt she could not do that but reiterated her earlier desire to work with David and suggested they work together. When David offered Mary an hourly rate for her work or a salary, Mary refused, saying she wanted to be part of the business or would not leave her current job. It became clear that David's business was outgrowing its sole proprietorship model. David asked Mary if she wanted to become a partner and Mary readily accepted.

Partnership

These business relationships also arise automatically when two or more people engage in an organized activity without specifying another structure to govern their association. The law presumes that partnership is intended where you engage in business with another principal even if you do not have a written understanding.

Partnerships can also be created by contract (probably a good idea) where two or more people decide to engage in a joint undertaking and want to specify the ground rules governing their working relationship. A simple form of partnership agreement is provided in Appendix B.

How To Form a Partnership

This business form is similar to sole proprietorship in that it arises automatically (or by agreement), provides for personal legal liability and tax responsibility to the partners and is simple to form and govern.

To create a partnership, two or more people merely begin to engage in the business. If there is considerable public contact or the desire to protect and preserve a trade name, a certificate of doing business should be filed as with a sole proprietorship. Please note this important caveat: **If there is no written partnership agreement, the law implies certain minimal understandings between the parties such as equal shares in profits and losses plus the potential for full responsibility for debts.**

Because the law may impose an understanding different from that contemplated by the parties, we strongly suggested that an agreement be created if you select the partnership mode.

Partnership agreements govern both the positive (share of profits, measure of control, etc.) and negative (percentage of liability for debts, restrictions of transferability, etc.) aspects of the working arrangement. Great care must be taken in drafting such a document.

Simple forms of partnership agreements are available from most large stationery stores and in a number of legal books, including Charles' *Legal Guide*, available from Crisp.

As with most legal arrangements carrying potential exposure, it is probably best to consult counsel. The following checklist should help assure that the agreement is complete:

Partnership Agreement Checklist

☐ What name will be used?

☐ How much capital contribution will each partner make and what percentage of ownership will he or she have?

☐ What are the functional responsibilities of each partner and how much control will each have (if less than an equal share)?

- [ ] If salaries (referred to as "draws" in partnerships) are to be taken, how much will each get and when?

- [ ] Are bonuses to be granted, and if so, by whom and when?

- [ ] How are profits and losses to be treated among the partners?

- [ ] Restrictions (if any) on other activities of partners (e.g., prohibition against competing with the partnership).

- [ ] Duration of the partnership and guidelines as to how the partnership is to be terminated.

- [ ] Provisions for distribution of partnership assets (including good-will, if any) upon dissolution. This clause should probably include a final accounting (maybe even independent audit).

- [ ] Clause regarding dispute resolution (we suggest mediation because of the nature of the relationship).

The Good News and the Bad News of Partnerships

As with sole proprietorships, the best news with partnerships is the ease of formation. This form of organization has potential tax benefits called "flow-through" whereby partners can deduct partnership losses and expenses against ordinary income. There is also no double taxation as with the corporate form.

Partnerships are ideal for close, trusting working relationships. They allow partners a wide range for power and control. They are also the perfect vehicle for joint and equal financial contribution and share in a venture.

The bad news also relates to the ease of formation. A partnership can come into existence even when it was not intended. Such ease of formation can cause problems when parties did not intend to be partners, or when one party binds another to an obligation or debt because the law implied a partnership from the working relationship.

Also on the bad news side is the difficulty in attracting nonpartner capital and lack of an entity to pass shares of stock openly and freely. The automatic termination provisions of the partnership law, which include dissolution upon the death (and in some states disability) of a partner, can be a negative factor, although a properly drawn agreement can get around the automatic dissolution.

Employee Issues of Partnerships

As with sole proprietorship, partners as employers are under the usual legal obligations of law to employees. With partnerships, it is important to distinguish between a partner and an employee. It may very well be that each intended that the worker be an employee, but because of unclarity about the working arrangement, the law treats him or her as a partner. This could mean that the worker might inadvertently waive a right to wages and even be held responsible for a share of the debts.

On the other hand, the worker might be entitled to a share of the profits if he or she is held to be a partner. You can provide for both of these contingencies in the partnership agreement. A clear, written understanding should exist between the employer (the partnership) and the employee that they have entered an employment arrangement and not a partnership agreement.

Tax Implications of Partnerships

We said under "good news" that partnerships can have very attractive tax benefits. This arises out of the fact that like a proprietorship, a partnership has no identity apart from its participants and is therefore taxed through its participants. Partners thus pay taxes at their own individual rates and may deduct their share of partnership losses and must declare their share of partnership profits.

The partnership, while not a legal entity for tax law or other liability purposes, must file a partnership return (IRS Form 1065), which the IRS uses for information purposes and not as the tax-collection vehicle. Payments to the IRS (or deductions from losses) are indicated by the partnership distributing to its partners Schedule K-1. Partners use this form as the worksheet when filling out their Schedule E (Supplemental Income Schedule) and their Form 1040 returns. Because the actual taxes due calculation are made at each partner's own tax rate, partners could end up paying different sums in taxes.

While the flow-through aspects of tax treatment of partnerships appears an attractive feature, as it usually is, you must also remember that your tax liability will be calculated on the profitability of the partnership regardless of whether it distributes cash. Thus, while the partnership may have had a good year, it may not want to distribute cash—but you may be liable to pay as if it did.

There are a number of other nuances to the tax laws that affect tax rates and deductibility of items for partners. These include such important factors as Social Security, which cannot be deducted (since partner draws are not wages), certain employee fringe benefits such as health and other insurance, and some other benefit plans that may not be deductible to the partners.

An important alert: the IRS will presume that any business that has several persons participating in it for profit and/or loss is a partnership for tax purposes. This is fine, if that is your intent. But if you are engaging in a joint activity that is not a partnership or a corporation, you better get some good tax advice. This should probably be a standard admonition to all partners except perhaps those involved in the simplest of partnership undertakings.

Limited Partnerships

We cannot leave a discussion of partnership without some comment about limited partnership. This entity has the same attributes as a general partnership but it has a unique feature that allows it to attract investors. Briefly stated, a limited partnership has one or more general partners and one or more limited partners. The general partners have the same liabilities, responsibilities and controls as described above, while the limited partners are liable only to the extent of their financial commitment to the firm. As long as they stay away from the day-to-day business of the firm, they are not liable for the general debts and obligations as if they were full, general partners. **The law is very strict about this and even requires limited partnerships to be registered (somewhat like corporations) in some states.**

You can see obvious benefits of this form where the general partners understand the business and the limited partners can provide financial support but aren't knowledgeable enough, or are unwilling to run the risks of the liability of general partners. In the past these forms provided tax benefits beyond the amount of invested capital and were very attractive tax shelters. Since tax reform, limited partners can only deduct as losses their legitimate share of the loss, bearing in mind the level of their risk. While the limited partnership can allocate profit or loss as it sees fit (as with any other partnership agreement), the IRS will now look very carefully at limited partners to assure that their deductions bear real relationship to their level of financial exposure or commitment in the deal.

Limited partnerships are still used to finance major projects such as real estate developments, energy production or exploration and motion pictures. The level of sophistication and need for carefully prepared legal documentation takes limited partnerships out of the mainstream of small business organization.

UPDATE ON DAVID'S CASE

After a year of operations, David Reuban Associates is really doing well. Mary is a 40% partner and earned a nice income on her share of the profits from the first year. David too was able to supplement his income by his draws from the firm, although he only took 40% of the profit in cash, leaving some cash in the firm for continuing operations.

It turns out the project David and Mary developed for the new firm was so successful, the multinational French-based firm that owned David's client approached David with a request that he develop new projects for their European operations.

David and Mary knew that they could not handle a project of this magnitude without adding creative staff, beefing up their equipment and bringing in a full-time administrator/business manager. David estimated that they needed at least one hundred thousand dollars of additional capital to go into

---

the business before they could take on such a major task with international travel and business. In fact, David, Mary and Phyllis (who served as an unpaid adviser to the business) estimated that they would have to spend more than fifty thousand dollars in new computer and communications equipment just to prepare for this undertaking.

The quandary was that their existing business was doing quite well and that Mary and David got along well themselves and with their part-time staff associate and bookkeeper. They knew eventually they would have to leave the comfortable offices in David's home and rent larger office space and, basically, add a lot of hassles to their relatively peaceful life.

However, as Phyllis pointed out, the potential profit from this new job was just too great to pass up. Besides, enough profit might be left over to attract an outside investor to finance this expansion.

After great deliberation and long hours of soul-searching, Mary and David agreed to go after the job. They contacted the bank for enough money to prepare the proposal properly. The bank wished the partners well but turned them down since the earlier loan to David and Phyllis was still unpaid (although all interest had been paid in a timely fashion).

At Phyllis's suggestion, David spoke to his father-in-law who had recently sold a home and received a substantial profit from it. His father-in-law also wished David well, but explained that the project was "out of his league." David's father-in-law mentioned a friend who might back the project for a share in the company but he would want no part of the operation. The friend, Ned, recently received a "golden parachute" to retire early and had fifty thousand dollars in discretionary funds he might be willing to risk.

David, Mary and Ned met at Phyllis's brother's law office. After discussing the different options for Ned's participation, David asked if he wanted to become a limited partner in the firm. Ned said that while he didn't want to run, or even be part of everyday operations, "he never invested in a business in which he did not have a say." He turned down the partnership because he didn't want to be liable for any firms debts. Ned asked if he could join David and Mary on the Board of Directors.

It appeared as if it was now time to incorporate David Reuban Associates.

Corporations

In assessing the best form of organization for your home business, be certain to contrast corporations to both sole proprietorships and partnerships. The principal difference between corporations and both sole proprietorships and partnerships is that the corporation has a legal status of its own independent of the people who work there, manage it or own it. You, as a businessperson, may be interested to know that this form of organization apparently grew out of the need to have an entity that had a life longer than a person and that had the ability to transact business on its own.[3]

Today, as every business person knows, existence of a corporation as a legal "person" is a well accepted legal fiction (meaning that a corporation is not a real person but the law has decided to give it certain personhood). In deciding what legal form best suits your business's financial needs, you should know that a far more complex set of legal issues has arisen around corporations than around either sole proprietorships or partnerships. And, again, while we remind you this is not a legal treatise, we will spend some more time discussing the background and requirements for operating in the corporate mode.

Because the corporation is a legal entity, separate and apart from its human owners or operators, it has its own legal capabilities and obligations. Among these are the ability to acquire, own or transfer property, the ability to engage in contractual undertakings it its own right and the power to hire and fire employees.

As noted in the discussion of raising capital in Chapter 6, ownership in the corporation is evidenced by what is called equity participation—that is, through shares. Investors can acquire shares in any fashion according to state law, including from cash, property, or services rendered. Shareholders in a corporation own the firm and have the right to elect directors. Directors appoint or elect officers who are responsible for running the company. Directors are responsible for the strategic or long-term decisions, while officers are responsible for the tactical or short-term needs of managing the firm.

How To Form a Corporate Home Business

Since the corporation, unlike the two prior entities, exists only by operation of law, its legal life depends completely upon state law (statutes). Each state has its own laws governing the formation, life, powers of and dissolution of corporate existence. Thus, to form a corporation, the parties intending to form it (called "promoters") must contact the official agency that handles corporate formation in the state and file the required forms. In most states, corporate formation is handled by the secretary of state or a distinct state division of corporations.

While most states will accept formation documents (called "articles or certificate of incorporation") that contain the minimum information shown in Appendix E, they prefer that their own recommended format be used. Many states provide pre-printed corporate organization forms and some are even sold in certain stationery and bookstores. Most states require a specialized suffix be used for the business name showing the legal nature of the organization, such as "incorporated," "Corporation" or "Inc."

In addition to the formality of written articles of incorporation, the state will require a natural person or company (usually residing in that state) to be an "agent for service of process." This person or firm agrees that if the corpora-

---

[3] (Hornstein, *Corporate Law and Practice*. St. Paul, MN. West Publishing Co. 1959. Pages 10–12)

tion is sued or the state makes an official communication to the corporation, they are legally complete by serving the statutory agent.

Each state charges a filing or registration fee and a tax on the shares either issued or authorized. This franchise tax may be calculated on the number of shares that the corporation wishes to authorize (i.e., will be able to issue). Please don't confuse "franchise tax" with "franchise fees" charged in business relationships between a franchiser and franchisee.

In addition to the formation fees and forms, the state agency having jurisdiction will require annual reports (from for-profit corporations) and an annual fee to remain in existence. Since the corporation exists only with the "permission" of the state, if fees are not paid or the corporation acts beyond its powers (called "ultra vires" by the lawyers), the state can revoke the corporate charter.

As stated above, one of the principal attributes of a corporation is its ability to continue to exist beyond the life of its incorporators (those who undertake the legal process of incorporation). The articles of incorporation will specify how long the corporation will exist. It can even be perpetual, which in law means that it will continue in existence until dissolved by operation of law or act of dissolution by its principals.

Good News and the Bad News of Corporations

If you decide that the corporate form best suits the financial and growth needs of your home business, be ready for good news—and bad news. The good news is the corporation's advantage over any other business form in its ability to continue to exist on its own. This allows your home business to develop its potential for special value. Because ownership of a corporation is evidenced by shares and the shares can be transferred (unless an agreement exists that prohibits such transfers), a corporation can raise money through sale of shares. Shares can also become a valuable asset in the estate planning of stock owners.

Perhaps the best news about a corporation is the insulation of individual business owners and operators from personal liability. Under both proprietorship and partnership, principals remain personally liable for the debts, obligations, and torts (noncontract wrongs such as accidents and negligence) of their businesses. This is not true of corporations. The corporation is a "legal person" for purposes of doing business and liable for its own debts. Shareholder obligations are limited to the amount of money he or she agreed to invest or lend to the company. While this sounds like a good way out of personal obligations, newer corporations or those with few assets will not usually qualify on their own for loans or other credit and may need their principals to sign personal guarantees. However, liability rests on the personal guaranty contract, not on the corporation.

Some business consultants refer to corporations as cheap insurance against personal liability. Businesses that have constant and continuing public contact or that sell a product or provide a service where a potential for legal liability to third persons exists should seriously consider the corporate form. Without the protection of a corporation, a principal could find him or herself sued personally after a mishap. Remember, however, our friend who owned the rental property and franchise who decided to retain the sole proprietorship model but obtain adequate insurance coverage.

Another important note on the corporate form and liability is in order here. While most of professions can now operate under a corporate umbrella (known in most states as "P.C.–Professional Corporations" or "P.A.–Professional Associations"), the corporate form cannot insulate such professionals from the special fiduciary liability they have to their constituency. Thus a home-based medical practice that is incorporated cannot shield a physician from malpractice, nor can lawyers, architects and certain others hide behind a corporation where they are negligent.

Now for the bad news of the corporate choice. A major negative factor is the possibility of double taxation for corporations. A regular cooperation is a person for tax-paying purposes. Thus, it may very well owe its own taxes in addition to the taxes individual shareholders have to pay on wages and dividends they receive.

Another disadvantage of corporations, especially for home business people who prefer a more casual method of doing business, is the necessity to comply with regulatory requirements both as to formation and to continuation of business in this form. Some states have periodic forms and returns that all resident corporations must file. A corporation formed in another state must qualify as a "foreign corporation" to do business in a state outside of its formation state.)

Companies that decide to sell their shares to the general public will have to register offerings of shares at the federal level if the offering is to be interstate. The agency governing such offers is the Securities and Exchange Commission (SEC). Registration requirements for the SEC are very stringent to protect the public from fraudulent share offers. Every state has its own securities registration requirements for intrastate offers. These laws (known as "Blue Sky Laws") vary from a simple informational filing to elaborate advance clearing by the agency similar to the SEC requirements. No company should even consider "going public" without the advice of qualified securities counsel and financial adviser.

Employee Issues of Corporations

With corporations, the company (however large or small) is the employer and must comply with the legal requirements of appropriate personal and financial treatment of employees. That's the good news side from an employer standpoint; however, most states require strict compliance with working conditions and other related laws and will "pierce the corporate veil" to snag individual officers or directors who violate these requirements. Remember always with a corporation, the ultimate power of the state is to close down the business. Even then, corporate officers who intentionally violate labor laws (including refusal or failure to pay wages) may be personally liable. Check with your own state labor department if this question is of concern to you.

Tax Implications of Corporations

For tax purposes, corporations are generally divided into two types: C-corporations (known usually as general business corporations) and S-corporations (known usually as a small business corporation). The size of the business has little bearing on which corporate form the principals elect. Rather, the number of shareholders and how they want to file taxes will dictate which form will be used. Thus, it is not fair to assume that a home business will always be an S-corp while a nonhome business will be a C-corp.

Generally speaking, a company that anticipates growth in operations and the need for more than one principal stockholder (or family members) elects to be treated as a C-corp. This means that both the corporation and shareholders will be taxed. Losses, if any, are reserved by the C-corp against future earnings and are not passed through to shareholders. The corporate tax rate should be checked for both federal and state corporate taxes, if any. Some states do not automatically tax corporate revenues, but have a franchise or doing business tax as an option.

Successful companies should be aware of special provisions of the federal corporation tax laws that govern how much capital the business can accumulate after payment of operating expenses including wages and taxes. Usually, a portion of what remains (after a reserve for anticipated upcoming financial needs) is passed along to shareholders as dividends and is taxable to them on their own returns. Because these dividends may not be deductible to the corporation and are taxable to the recipient, double taxation results. One answer to this problem where the shareholder is also an operating employee is to pay a larger salary, which would be taxed as part of the employee's personal tax obligation but would be deductible by the corporation as an operating expense. The additional income is thus additional wage, and not subject to double taxation.

A corporation can be used in some cases to provide very nice fringe benefits and individual perks. While rules on deductibility of certain expenses have been tightened recently, corporate use of a car, business entertaining or travel and expenses for some job-related educational courses should still be obtainable relatively tax-free. Retirement, medical and hospitalization, profit-sharing and other financial security benefits may also have very attractive tax consequences for the shareholder. You should consult your tax professional for details on what perks the corporation may pay for, deduct as corporate expenses and what of such benefits may be taxable to you as income.

Where the business has primarily one or few shareholders (closely held), as with many home businesses, a Small Business Corporation (formerly referred to as Subchapter S Corporation and now knows as an "S-corp") may be the answer. S-corps have been called corporations treated like individuals for tax purposes. They have similar tax flow-through provisions as partnerships and proprietorships. Shareholders of S-corps have the same shelter from liability but are not subject to the double taxation possibilities of C-corps.

Since S-corps have special tax treatment, some strict rules govern this type of business. These firms are formed legally the same way any other corporation is formed. Soon after the business begins to function, the owners request S-corp tax treatment by filing IRS Form 2553 with the IRS office for the area in which the corporation is located. The IRS will inform applicants as to whether or not they meet the S-corp guidelines.

You own tax adviser can provide details about complying with S-corp guidelines (which are, in essence, restrictions on corporate structure). In general, to qualify as an S-corp, the firm must be a United States (domestic) corporation. The corporation may only have one class of stock with no more than 35 shareholders who must be natural persons (not corporations or partnerships). Every shareholder must be either a United States citizen or legal resident. Domestic international service corporations (DISCs) don't qualify, nor do banks, insurance companies, companies receiving special Puerto Rico tax credit or members of what the IRS calls "affiliated groups."

While S-corps don't have to pay corporate income taxes, they are required (like partnerships) to file information returns. The S-corp furnishes shareholders with information which is then reported on the individual shareholder's own tax return.

Several important caveats are in order with regard to S-corps. These are creatures of federal tax laws. Your own state tax people may not share the federal government's view about S-corp treatment and tax these corporations just like any other corporation. Also, since S-corps are very much like privileged entities under the federal corporation tax laws, rules as to their treatment are tightly enforced. In other words, even though S-corp treatment may be initially approved by the IRS, that status can be lost if the corporation engages in what the IRS believes is activity not consistent with S-corp guidelines.

Because of the complexities of corporate tax laws relating to both C and S corporations, we strongly recommend consultation with your tax professional. You should first contact your neighborhood IRS office and request copies of tax returns and information sheets on partnerships, C-corps and S-corps and compare the reporting and payment requirements. Then, if possible, speak to someone who operates a home business or practice in each form and ask about their views of the tax issues and considerations.

UPDATE ON DAVID'S CASE

In fact, David, Mary and Ned formed a corporation called Damyn Company, Inc. ("DCI"). They retained the corporate headquarters in David's home but also opened an office in downtown Washington, D.C.

In spite of some early stumbles and the usual new business pitfalls, DCI found itself doing quite well. An attractive addition to the house provided ample, efficient work space and additional consultants could be called in on an adjunct basis as needed.

> Soon, an Italian electronics firm approached David to help introduce a new personal paging device into the United States market. David and Mario (a principal of the Italian firm) thought about forming a new company to market jointly the device in the United States.
>
> David called counsel (no longer Phyllis's brother but an independent corporate and international law specialist) who suggested a joint venture.

Joint Venture

A joint venture is an undertaking by two or more persons or organizations to share the expense and profit of a particular project. You can use this device whenever something needs to be done, needs resources or needs input beyond your own capability, but that does not necessarily require forming a business organization to undertake it.

How To Form a Joint Venture

Joint ventures are not business organizations in the sense of proprietorships, partnerships or corporations, although they can be partnerships between firms. They are, usually, agreements between parties or firms for a particular purpose or venture. Their formation may be very informal, such as a handshake and an agreement for two firms to share a booth at a trade show; however, joint venture arrangements can also be very complex, such as the consortium of major United States electronics firms to develop new microchips.

Joint ventures are governed by the agreement that brings them into being. Unless the creation of a corporation or partnership formalizes the joint venture, it never ripens into a tax-paying, legal entity on its own but, instead, functions through the legal status of the venture participants (known as co-venturers or venture partners). A joint venture is essentially a form of partnership limited to a particular purpose. Many times, joint ventures take on a formalized partnership form.

Because the joint venture is not usually a legal entity on its own, it does not hire people, enter into contracts or have its own tax liabilities. These matters are handled through the coventurers. Contract law, not corporate law, partnership law, or the law of sole proprietorship governs joint ventures.

ON YOUR OWN

- After considering the legal ramifications and implications of doing business on your own, do you still want to?

- Which of the various forms of business organization seems best suited to your personal, business and long-term needs?

- Are you prepared to deal with the various legal requirements and other regulatory and procedural requirements of your own home business?

- Is there an adviser or experienced home business person you can talk to who can help you make good decisions about business organization and structure in view of the specialized needs of your home-based business?

CHAPTER V.

Evaluating and Protecting Home Business Assets

"if it ain't broke, don't fix it . . .
unless it's obsolete."

—Anonymous

GENERAL PROTECTION AND INSURANCE

A business is only as solid as its assets. This statement is true whether the prime assets are inanimate tangible things such as antiques, intangibles such as computer software or living things such as human beings (i.e., a physician). In any of these cases, the business must be certain that its assets are protected. No financial institution, potential business partner or professional colleague will think much of any business, home-based or otherwise, that does not have a sufficient sense of self-worth to take steps to protect its assets.

When discussing assets we consider their acquisition, physical protection, and legal and insurance protection.

Elsewhere in the book (Chapter 3) we talk about planning for the business financing needs of your company including acquisition of assets. The need for physical security, while not obvious, is something you will address when ensuring that your home business has adequate fire and theft protection. Thus, in addition to those organizational items listed in Appendix D, consider where the home workspace is located. If it is on the basement or first floor and easy to break into, you might give serious consideration to an electronic security alarm system.

Insuring both the business assets and the business itself from loss and even interruption by an emergency is essential to your asset protection program. Don't assume that your homeowner's policy will automatically cover home business losses. The best thing is to be open about your plans and consult your insurance agent. After all, should you experience a loss and a need for insurance and the company turns down your coverage for failure to disclose the business use of the premises, wouldn't you be sorry you tried to save a few premium dollars?

Let's now take a closer look at some of the more creative assets of the business, and give some concentrated thought to the value they may have to you and the business and consider how best to legally preserve and protect them.

INTELLECTUAL PROPERTY OF THE BUSINESS

We're sure you would agree that business, home-based or not, could not take place without some mechanism to protect new ideas, trade secrets, processes, designs, writings or other works representing the product of the creative mind or intellect. The field of law covering the legal protection of innovation is called "intellectual property law" and is considered a subset of commercial law. Often, practitioners are specialists who have backgrounds in both law and the technical area of innovation.

While intellectual property law is very technical and invites the assistance of a lawyer specially versed in the particular topic, any person involved in a business or profession calling upon research and development or other innovative thinking aimed at offering a new or distinctive product or service needs some important general knowledge about this field. Home-based business people are often the most creative and innovative—they have to be to compete with the big firms. Every businessperson should know what his or her opportunities and mechanisms are for protecting these kinds of property rights and also what obligations you have for not infringing upon the legal rights of others.

Intellectual property law involves a compendium of federal and state laws, administrative regulations and court decisions. What follows is a very general outline of the various individual areas in the field known as intellectual property law. Much of the information for this section comes from Charles' *Legal Guide*.

PATENT PROTECTION

What Is Patent Protection?

A patent is the legal means by which a government grants to an inventor a "statutory monopoly" (which in the United States amounts to seventeen years) for any "new and useful process, machine, manufacture, or composition of matter, or any new and useful improvement thereof." If is presumed that the grant of a legal monopoly will stimulate development and innovation.

Certain unique and distinctive designs can also receive a patent. Design patents give "ornamental protection" for three and a half, seven, or fourteen years, as the applicant may choose. The patent grant prohibits anyone else from practicing that invention or using that design for the life of the patent. Anyone who does infringe violates both civil and criminal proscriptions.

What Is Patentable?

Patents protect the innovative idea. If you look at the quote above from the Patent Act, you will see that patent protection may be available for processes, machines, manufacturing process, composition of matter (including chemical formulae), and "new and useful" improvements. We have learned in recent years that patents can also be issued for plants, certain software algorithms and genetically engineered animals. These categories are often referred to as the "subject matter" of patents.

In addition to being appropriate subject matter, an invention to be patented must be "useful." This has been quite loosely construed to mean "having some utilitarian value." The invention must also be able to be "reduced to practice." This means that the Patent and Trademark Office (PTO) examiner must be able to see that the invention is more than pure theory. It must be capable of being produced. Thus, the concept for a new bridge could be patented without building the full-sized bridge if the inventor can demonstrate through a model or otherwise that the invention can be practiced (i.e., used).

To receive a patent, the invention must be new. That means it cannot have been used before or have been published. Disclosure to the public would put it into the public domain. This requirement is quite strict. If a professor develops a new theory and writes a paper about it that is then published, he or she cannot later apply for a patent. The person actually applying for the patent must have created the invention. There is an important distinction here between assignability of the patent (once issued) and assignability of the right to apply. An inventor cannot transfer his or her idea to someone else who then applies for the patent. This is considered fraudulent conduct and could result in consequences far worse than mere rejection of the patent application.

Sometimes the real inventor creates something for someone else. We know of a professional inventor whose full-time home-based business is to invent and design for others from his home lab. In such a case, there is a need to assign the legal rights in the invention to another. This is done after the real inventor applies for the patent and is available to pursue ("Prosecute") the application. We will comment later on how others can obtain rights to intellectual property.

An invention that meets all of the requirements discussed above will allow the application process to proceed but this does not guarantee that a patent will issue.

How To Apply for a Patent

The PTO maintains forms and procedures for proper application. It is possible to prepare and file your own application, but we strongly encourage you to obtain the services of a patent attorney or agent. In any event, the application process involves the following basic steps:

1. The inventor prepares and files the appropriate application and pays the necessary filing fees.

2. The PTO assigns the file (referred to by patent attorneys as "case") to an examiner, who reviews the materials and compares them with earlier patents and other materials (known as "prior art").

3. The report of the initial review is often a rejection with grounds stated.

4. The applicant (through counsel usually) then files an amended application with changes.

5. The application is then granted a letters patent with a number and fancy certificate (or is rejected again for further work).

Note: During the period of time between filing the application and the patent grant, an applicant is permitted to use the term "patent pending." This important provision gives the public notice that an application for protection has been made to the PTO. Thus, if you are in the process of filing a patent application, you can immediately mark your goods with the term "patent pending." Keep in mind that the law calls for a fine for misuse of this term to prevent abuse of this process.

While awaiting your patent, be patient. The PTO receives more than 100,000 applications each year from all over the world.

Assuming that a patent is granted, let's look next at what the inventor actually gets.

The Nature of the Rights in a Patent

It is very important to understand the nature of the rights obtained by the inventor from the PTO. A patent is not an exclusive permission to "practice" the patent. Instead, it prohibits people other than the duly registered inventor (or inventors) to practice the invention. In other words, a patent gives the inventor the right to stop someone else from violating this statutory monopoly (violation is called "infringement").

Note that the issuance of a patent is not automatic permission to use the technology to make something. Suppose, for example, that you develop a new formula for a type of insecticide, but current environmental laws forbid use of that product. This means that even if a patent were to issue, the inventor could not practice it without complying with other legal requirements.

As stated earlier, the whole purpose of a patent originally was to stimulate economic development and is only available to inventions the inventor does not "abandon." In this context, abandonment means failure to pursue patent application rights within a reasonable amount of time. This can be shown by express act of the inventor or implied from his or her conduct.

Enforcing Legal Rights

Because a patent grants the right to prevent infringement, a closure look at "infringement" and the legal rights of the inventor follow.

It would seem as if the right to exclusively practice an invention through a patent ought to be clear and without confusion. After all, before a patent issues, a highly qualified examiner, usually very familiar with the other items available in the field, reviews the case and decides whether to allow a patent. If he or she is aware of no other invention of the sort, he or she will recommend that a patent be granted.

Infringement refers to the unlawful usurpation of an individual's (or firm's) exclusive rights to commercially exploit or otherwise practice the invention. It can take a number of forms, but usually involves copying or otherwise "ripping off" or "knocking off" the product without permission to do so. Infringement can be domestic (i.e., from within the United States) or it can be foreign (non-United States manufactured goods that violate patent rights entering the United States).

When you feel your patent has been infringed, you have two options: You can seek an injunction, or you can sue for damages. Often, other remedies are requested in a federal patent infringement suit. Suits under the patent laws are brought in federal district courts. If the infringement is foreign, apply to the United States Trade Commission in Washington, D.C., for an order excluding the product from entry into the United States.

Great care and good legal advice are strongly advised before any decision is made to respond to allegations of patent infringement. Very often suits alleging patent infringement are countered with allegations that the patent is not valid (i.e., never should have been issued in the first place). Sometimes, these counter-claims prevail and the original patentee (patent holder) loses all patent protection.

Some attorneys and other commentators refer to a patent as nothing more than a "fighting interest in a lawsuit." Whether or not this is true, if the infringer has the resources to countersue, the litigation may not be worth engaging in the first place. Of course, we would suggest mediation as a reasonable alternative to almost any lawsuit, especially one where technology and innovation is an issue.[1]

Often, patent owners consider granting licenses to alleged infringers as part of the process of enforcing the rights. At least, there will be some financial consideration for the infringement under this model. I remember a corporate client from my lawyering days who refused to grant a license to a Taiwanese firm that wanted to manufacture a popular tool sold on United States television. The client had a United States patent, but that did not deter the rejected Taiwanese company from knocking off the project. We stopped them eventually, but by then, they had sold as much product as my client had sold and they had gone out of

---

[1] Charles has a new publication on the use of "alternatives" in technology, intellectual property and innovation-based disputes. Lickson, Charles. "Use of ADR in Intellectual Property, Technology and Innovation-Based Disputes," 55 *AmJur Trials* 483. Rochester, NY. Lawyers Cooperative Publishing. 1995.

business in the United States. Our victory, which cost the client many thousands of dollars, was important as a warning to others, but empty in real financial terms.

If enforcing patents is so expensive and may not result in a positive outcome, why bother getting a patent? Many firms don't bother. They just hope to get to the market first and use quality and advertising as their resource for their market share. Other firms, especially larger firms with in-house patent counsel and/or substantial financial resources, are prepared to fight to prevent infringement. Obviously, if you have developed a distinctive and potentially patentable product, you will weigh the advantages against the costs and other disadvantages before deciding whether to apply for a patent . . . and by all means, seek competent legal advice before applying for a patent.

COPYRIGHT PROTECTION OF PROPERTY

You noted from the discussion on patents above that in general, patents protect the idea. It follows that copyright protects the manifestation of an idea, not the idea itself. Thus, if an author writes a book, the ideas expressed in the book are not in themselves protected. Rather, the actual words, phrases and structure—i.e., the physical manifestation of the book's ideas—receive copyright protection.

Copyright protection is based on federal laws and, like patent laws, gives the owner exclusive rights to:

- Reproduce and distribute the protected work

- To prepare a derived work based on the copyright protected original

- Perform or display the copyrighted work publicly

How To Obtain Copyright Protection

Application for copyright protection is made on Form TX provided by the Register of Copyrights, Copyright Office at the Library of Congress, Washington, D.C. 20559. When this form is filed together with the appropriate fee and two copies of the work are sent in, there is a presumption that the copyright issued. Unlike patent application, copyright applications are not subject to extensive review, searches and clearances. In essence, review is made only when another person contends that a copyright should not issue. (Grounds for objecting to an application for copyright include allegations that the work in question infringes upon someone else's rights or that the author claimed is not the real author.)

To symbolize your copyright protection and comply with some of the international copyright conventions, notice of your copyright claim should be uniform. The symbol © or the word "Copyright" followed by the year of creation and the name of the owner is sufficient. Although it is not legally required, we usually add the words: "All rights reserved" (which used to be required for certain international protection). Now, we use these words as further evidence of my determination to protect our rights. Thus, you will see on our written materials the following: "Copyright 1996 Charles P. and Bryane M. Lickson. All rights reserved."

The term of protection commences at the time the work is created and continues for the life of the author plus fifty years.[2] The term is slightly longer for "works for hire" where someone is asked to create something under contract. That term is the life of the author plus seventy-five years, or one hundred years from creation (whichever is shorter). Thereafter, as with patent ideas, the copyright reverts to the public domain.

An important distinction must be made between patents and copyrights in how the protection is derived. In patents, you must file a formal application before protection or legal rights ensure. Not so with copyrights. The rights actually begin upon the creation of the work. In fact, one need never apply for a federal copyright to have a copyright. The "common-law copyright" gives the author the right to stop anyone else from taking his or her copyrighted materials. State courts can be used for these personal rights. Of course, proving the case might be quite difficult. A filing with the Copyright Office gives the copyright holder access to federal courts and some documentation of his or her rights. In federal court, the copyright owner can also be awarded attorneys' fees and even seek punishment against an intentional infringer.

Who Owns the Copyright?

While the answer to this question ought to be easy, it is not. The question poses problems not only for the general public, but also for practitioners of intellectual property law. The question becomes even more difficult if an "outsider" is hired to create a work for remuneration.

A landmark 1989 United States Supreme Court decision relating to the United States Copyright Act's "work made for hire" provisions is *Community for Creative Non-Violence, ("CCNV") et al. v. Reid*, No. 88-293 (June 5, 1989). This case is very important for home-based artists, craftspeople and others who create new works themselves or for others. The CCNV case confirms the importance of using carefully prepared written assignment agreements with both independent contractors and employees who are engaged in creative development services. Although the work in this case was a copyrightable work (i.e., a work of art), the assignment you or your attorney prepares should cover other intellectual property rights as well.

Unfortunately, in the *CCNV* case, the Supreme Court did not create clear criteria for when someone is considered an "employee," but rather left it to a subjective test on a case-by-case basis. This means that litigation over ownership of a newly developed work could arise when no agreement exists that delineates such rights, particularly in the "independent contractor" situation. As a practical

---

[2] Copyright Act, January 1, 1978.

matter, the only way a company can ensure that it owns the work of an "independent contractor" is pursuant to a formal written assignment agreement.

Because of the possibilities that you might undertake in your home business a "work for hire," let's take a more detailed look at "Work Made for Hire Provisions" of the United States Copyright Act (the "Act"). Section 101 defines a "work made for hire" as:

(1) a work prepared by an employee within the scope of his or her employment; or

(2) a work specially ordered or commissioned for use

    [a] as a contribution to a collective work,
    [b] as a part of a motion picture or other audiovisual work,
    [c] as a translation,
    [d] as a supplementary work,
    [e] as a compilation,
    [f] as an instructional text,
    [g] as a test,
    [h] as answer material for a test, or
    [i] as an atlas,

If the parties expressly agree in a written instrument signed by them that the work shall be considered a work made for hire.

Also important to note is Section 201(b) of the Act which provides that the employer or other person for whom a work made for hire was prepared is considered the "author" of the work for copyright purposes.

Under the definition of Section 101, to qualify as a "work made for hire," a work must either be prepared by an employee within the ordinary scope of employment under agency rules, or must fall into one of the categories of commissioned works *and* be subject to a written agreement between the parties that classify the work as a work made for hire.

Despite the language of the Act, a number of different interpretations of the meaning of "employee" have emerged in the case law. Several courts adopted what they call a "literal" interpretation. Under the strictest version of the literal interpretation, in order to be an "employee," the party creating the work must be a legitimate, salaried employee of the party requesting that the work be prepared.

Under the second major interpretation, courts have construed the word "employee" to include more than just formal salaried employees within agency law rules. Under this theory, even an independent contractor could be considered an "employee" if the independent contractor "were sufficiently supervised and directed by the hiring party."

The Supreme Court decision in the CCNV case raises serious questions about the ability to engage in creative work and applicability of the "works for hire" provision. This case is not only significant but also interesting and worth a closer look.[3] In 1985, Community for Creative Non-Violence, et al. ("CCNV") entered into an oral agreement with Reid, a sculptor, to produce a statue dramatizing the plight of the homeless. After the statue was completed and delivered, the parties filed competing copyright registration certificates. The agreement between Reid and CCNV made no mention of copyright rights. The federal district court held the sculpture was a "work made for hire" by an "employee" and, therefore, was owned exclusively by CCNV. The United States Court of Appeals reversed, holding the sculpture was not a "work made for hire" since it was not "prepared by an employee within the scope of his or her employment." That court looked at the sculptor's status as an "independent contractor" under the subsection of the "work made for hire" definition because "sculpture" is not one of the nine defined categories of works and the parties had not agreed in writing that the sculpture would be a work for hire.

On appeal, the Supreme Court, decided that general common-law agency principles must be first applied to determine whether the work was prepared by an employee or an independent contractor. Depending upon the outcome of that determination, the court would apply either the "employee" (clause (1)) or "independent contractor" (clause (2)) subsection in Section 101. Although the Act does not define "employee," "employment," or related terms, the court took the position that Congress meant them in their settled, common-law sense. Moreover, according to the Supreme Court, the general common-law of agency must be relied on, rather than the law of any particular state, since the Act expressly intends to create a federal law of uniform, nationwide application.

In this case, the court found the sculpture in question not to be a "work for hire," because the sculptor was an independent contractor rather than an "employee." Although CCNV directed enough of the work to ensure that the artist's work met its specifications, all other facts weighted heavily against finding an employment relationship.

On another issue, the court did not decide whether CCNV is a joint author of the sculpture and, thus, a co-owner of the copyright. The federal district court was directed to determine if the parties prepared the work with the intention of merging their contributions into inseparable or interdependent parts of a unitary whole.

It should be apparent from the Supreme Court's holding in the CCNV case that firms or individuals engaged in research and development as well as artistic endeavors should implement a carefully prepared written assignment agreement with both independent contractors and employees to avoid litigation over both the work for hire and co-ownership provisions of the Act. Such assignments should cover all types of intellectual property, and not merely copyrightable works.

---

[3] For the discussion of the CCNV case, the authors wish to acknowledge the Newsletter prepared by the Law Offices of Fenwick, Davis & West, Palo Alto, CA, for its valuable contribution to understanding of this important case.

TRADEMARK PROTECTION

In this day of mass communication, trademarks have become almost as significant a part of a product's identification as what the product does. Certain well-known trademarks have much value on their own, which has led to cross-licensing of marks. Names like "Coke," "Avon," "Radio Shack," "Cell Tech," "Xerox" and "Pepsi", all registered marks, automatically trigger identification with goods or services. If your home business has now or will have a distinctive name or mark for its goods and services, you may very well want to protect it as you would patent the invention or copyright the operating manual. Let's look first at what constitutes a protectable mark or name.

The mark, symbol or name must be unique and not used by anyone else in the same class of goods or services. This is quite a challenge, considering the many names, marks and symbols already in use. Advertising agencies and other creative resources can help.

The mark cannot be an unmodified generic noun or phrase. "Becky's Place" could become a tradename, but "Place" alone could not.

The mark must be used. If you have developed a distinctive mark, logo, design or other device for the purpose of using it to identify a product or service with you, you must do so. Thus, that wonderfully designed logo created by the Laura Little Studio for the new product you plan to bring out next year . . . maybe, cannot receive trademark protection until it is, in fact, used. However, you still have protection before you use a mark. Remember, you have at least a common-law copyright on the writing. Also, the law allows some time for bringing the product or service to market. In fact, the revised Trademark Act of 1988 even lets you apply for trademark registration prior to use so long as you confirm your intention actually to use the mark in commerce.

Do you have to register your mark? No. Like the automatic protection afforded copyrights when the material is created, a trademark can become proprietary by the mere fact of use in connection with a product or service. If you can prove that a trademark is yours, the courts will usually stop someone else from using it and may even award damages for the other's misuse. Some people use the initials "TM" to indicate their claim of a trademark or "SM" for service mark protection. These can be done without any legal proceedings. Be certain not to infringe someone else's mark!

Registration of the mark at the Patent and Trademark Office is recommended for certain practical reasons. Among the advantages of registration are the notice given through the PTO Gazette to all others of your claim in the mark. It also allows you to use the ® mark in connection with the name which acts as a warning to others not to infringe your rights in the mark.

The revised Trademark Act lowered the protection period for a mark from twenty years to ten years because so many people and firms registered marks and then abandoned them. So long as you are using the mark, you may seek protection for an initial period of ten years with subsequent renewal periods of ten years.

A quick note is in order on the distinction (sometimes confusion) between trademarks and service marks. Put simply, a trademark is associated with products and a service mark with service. Charles' firm Mediate-Tech, Inc. provides an example. The term "MTI Mediation" is a service mark used to describe our own mediation process; whereas "MTI Press" is a trademark we use to identify the printed material and audio tapes we offer.

TRADE SECRET PROTECTION

Most of the mechanisms described above to preserve a property interest in the intellectual property of your firm involve disclosing to a governmental agency the details of the item. Suppose you feel a product or process is confidential and proprietary, but you would rather not disclose how it is made. Can you protect it? What if, like David Reuban, you engage in creative work for others based upon your agreement of confidentiality? Can you preserve the integrity and confidentiality of the work done?

Yes, if the information can be kept secret. The formula for Coca-Cola and the recipe for Kentucky Friend Chicken have never been patented (presumably because such legal action would involve disclosing what the suppliers see as secret information).

A business trade secret must meet the following general requirements: (1) it must be considered as giving the firm some type of competitive advantage, (2) management must treat it as confidential information, and (3) it must be information not generally known outside the firm.

Note that this kind of protection is generally obtained by contract. Thus, you preserve your secrecy by having employees and others sign an agreement to keep the information private and confidential. A form of confidentiality agreement is available in the *Legal Guide* and from any lawyer.

In order to get a court to assist you in the preservation of company confidential or trade secret information, you must be able to show the court that you have taken every reasonable step possible to keep the information private and confidential. The following checklist should help you keep your business confidential information preserved for your firm's own use only.

Business Confidentiality Checklist

☐ Have I/we prepared confidentiality or nondisclosure agreements?

☐ Are all colleagues/consultants/employees who access confidential information required to sign?

☐ Are outsiders who are given access to confidential information required to sign a nondisclosure form?

☐ Is information that is to be considered confidential marked and clearly delineated as such?

☐ Is confidential information treated as such inside the firm?

☐ Have I/we taken reasonable steps to restrict access to confidential information?

☐ Do I/we have (or do I/we need) a policy regarding confidentiality and secrecy of certain information?

Another issue to be aware of while in your home business is to avoid having yourself accused of taking someone else's information. The best way of doing that is by being clear and careful about the information you will receive from outsiders.

Most firms will not even accept submissions of ideas from outsiders without a signed waiver of some type of limitation to the submitter to rights under the patent laws alone.

Trade secret protection is both easy and difficult. It is easy in that no formal outside filing, forms or registration is required with any state agency or any entity outside your own organization. It is difficult in that in order to establish that someone else violated your rights you must show that the information meets all the requirements outlined above and that you did your best to restrict access.

- Assess and evaluate the names, marks, logos and other identifiers that distinguish your company, product or service from all others.

- Determine whether your mark or name is generic or specific, even creative. The more creative, the greater the chance for protectability, registration approval at the PTO and enforceability against someone else using the mark.

- Consider adding the proprietary claiming initials "TM" and/or "SM" where appropriate.

- Give serious consideration to registering your mark at the PTO if it represents, in your view, a major asset or identifier for the firm.

- Review your own firm's information to determine what information or company data, if any, should be treated as confidential.

- With regard to this information, has it been marked appropriately and have reasonable steps been taken to preserve the confidentiality of such information?

- Do you need an employee confidentiality form?

- What is your procedure to protect confidentiality of information with regard to outsiders, including vendors?

- Does your firm accept ideas from outsiders (or employees) and if so, what is the arrangement regarding the confidentiality of such information?

It is now up to you to decide what innovative services, products, goods, information, names, marks, logos or data is of value to you and your home business. We have reviewed a variety of ways to protect intellectual property assets. It is now up to you to decide which to choose and what you will do to preserve these valuable business property rights.

CHAPTER VI.

Funding Sources (Where is the Money?)

Question: "Willie, why do you rob banks?"
Answer: "Because that's where the money is!"
—Willie Sutton

So, now you have finished your planning and are ready to launch (or are already well under way) your home business. As we have pointed out, sufficient capital is an absolute precondition to success. "Sufficient capital" in this context means more than you think you will need.

This chapter addresses where and how will you get that capital. The first hint as to the answer rests with that notable American—Willie Sutton—quoted above. You too must go where the money is. We divide sources of money into three categories: traditional, nontraditional, and government-related programs. It probably makes sense to start with a rundown of traditional sources.[1]

TRADITIONAL FUNDING SOURCES

Let's take a quick look at each of these traditional sources:

1. The business principals (yourself)

2. Others close to you (family and friends)

3. The business itself (your own firm)

---

[1] For purposes of this section, we borrow from Max Fallek's *Finding Money For Your Small Business*. Chicago, IL. Enterprise Dearborn. 1994.

4. Commercial banks

5. Savings and loan institutions

6. Loan companies

7. Insurance companies, pension funds and unions

8. Credit unions

9. Individual private investors

10. Institutional private investors (venture capitalists)

The Business Principal(s)

For the principal player in your home business, the most logical place to look for financing is in your own assets. These sources include money in bank accounts, certificates of deposit, stocks and bonds, cash value in insurance policies, real estate, home equity, coins, art or other valuable hobby collections, automobiles, boats, campers, pension fund, 401(K), Keogh or IRAs.

You might say that if you had sufficient capital, you would not need to turn to other sources. And you will recall the banker's paradox: the best risk is the person who doesn't need the money. But most sophisticated entrepreneurs know that to succeed, you must know how to use other people's money to finance the new or expanding business.

A work of caution about "plastic credit." These days, with banks so aggressive about their credit card distribution, most of us have one or more credit cards. It seems so easy (perhaps too easy) to take advantage of the availability of money simply by using these cards. ATM machines are everywhere and you probably have some checks that you can write on that credit card account for cash advances. Be alert that cash advances represent big (and very profitable) business for the credit card companies. They usually advance money at a much higher rate of interest than you would normally pay a bank or other financing source. And don't let the low monthly payment fool you. Although it may appear small, because of the high interest, your debt compounds and rises quickly. Soon you may be at your credit limit—or even beyond.

Watch out also for the check overdraft programs available from some banks. Because you can just write a check whether or not you have the money in the bank (up to the limit of your personal credit line), it may be too easy and too tempting to use this method. This may be a good source for extra financing (based on your own credit only), but interest may be costly. **Remember that until the tax laws change, interest paid on personal rather than real estate loans is not tax deductible**. You might consider a home-equity line of credit from a tax standpoint. As with all tax questions, consult your tax professional before making a decision.

Family

Another popular source of business capital is family. In some families, close (or even distant) relatives may have discretionary funds they can advance to your business. Unfortunately, money can easily get in the way of good family relationships. Use extreme care in determining whether to approach a family member about a financial participation in the business.

One approach that might help is to tell the relative about what you are doing and that there may be a need (or opportunity) for outside financial participation. They may have a genuine interest in doing so and might even resent the fact that you went to a stranger or conventional financing source without first giving them an opportunity to "get into the deal." The ideal way to have family participation in the funding is for them to ask to be involved.

The next challenge is to outline in a written document stringent guidelines about the terms and conditions of the arrangement. The quickest way to family trouble is to have an unwritten "gentlemen's agreement" about this financial transaction. In our mediation practice and training, we have seen firsthand the depth of conflict that can arise when family financial relationships go sour.[2]

The written guideline document between you and your relative(s) over the money for the business should be as detailed as possible so no one misunderstands each person's intentions in the matter. Among items to include are the following:

- Date of the loan

- When you get the money

- What form the money will take

- Loan amount

- Interest rate

- Due date of the loan

- Dates of loan payments

- Frequency of payments

- Collateral, if any

- What happens upon default

- Signatures of both parties

---

[2] An excellent resource for family business issues is Dr. Marshall Northington's *Managing The Family Business* (Crisp Publications). If you want to learn more about the potential for disarray in family (and other) conflict and how to resolve these difficult issues, you might want to read Charles' book *Ironing It Out: Seven Simple Steps to Resolving Conflict* (recently publsihed in a second edition from Crisp).

Of course, if a relative becomes the funding source you probably have greater incentive to repay than if money comes from any other place; however, give serious thought to what will happen if you default. Ideally, the relative is in the financial position to absorb the loss without serious downside effects. If we were to ask a relative for money for a business, besides the more formal legal loan understanding, we would also want a written statement that the person(s) knows the risks, can absorb the loss if that should happen and that the personal relationship will not be affected by failure of the financial transaction.

Friends

We agree with Max Fallek that the old adage "don't mix business with pleasure" is very relevant when thinking about bringing friends into financial transactions regarding the business. The truth is, friends can represent an excellent source of money needed for a small business start-up or to boost expansion of an ongoing business. When borrowing from friends, exercise the same caution you would in dealing with family. The kind of documentation referred to above would also apply regarding friends as a financial resource. Do whatever you can to make sure the financial transaction will not result in the loss of friendship.

The Business Itself

If you already have a home business and are in need of expansion money rather than seed or launch capital, one of the first places to turn is the business itself. An established business may have a number of financial options available. These include taking a first or second mortgage on any real estate or property that it owns, borrowing money against equipment or other fixed (hard) assets such as motor vehicles, borrowing against soft (intangible) assets such as copyrights if they have readily ascertainable value, borrowing against a pension fund, or borrowing against inventory or product or merchandise which could be sold if necessary.

Some other business loan support sources are:

Pledging Accounts Receivable

Money owed to the business but not yet received is a clear asset and should be available as collateral for a loan. When pledging accounts receivable, you exchange your legal right to get 100% of the money owed at some later date for less than 100% now. The lesser percent is based upon the calculation: money advanced less the cost of that money (i.e., interest and other charges if any).

When we refer to pledging we mean that your receivables are legally turned over to the bank or loan company that makes the loan. As the client or customer pays these receivables, the business deducts a certain amount of each payment until the loan is paid.

Factoring

Factoring is another way of using your receivables to raise needed cash. In factoring, you go to a factoring company, which actually buys your accounts receivable. It then receives the right to get the money directly from the client or customer.

Assume, for example, that consulting clients owe David Reuban $25,000 for work all agree was adequately performed. The companies that owe the money are on a thirty to sixty-day payment cycle but David needs to buy a new computer and to pay salaries now. He sells the receivables to the factor, who then owns the receivables. Of course, the factor gives David less than one hundred cents on the dollar. Its revenue comes from collecting the one hundred cents from David's accounts. The amount of discount that the factor takes depends on such things as how old the accounts receivable are, the credit rating of the debtor (David), what David did for the money, and even David's business's rating and reputation.

Factors will charge dearly for their services but are an important financial resource. They can take the form of organizations (like General Electric Credit Corp.) or individuals. You will find them in your telephone directory classified section under "factors" or through most more sophisticated banks.

Commercial Banks

When it comes to commercial or business loans, we normally think of a bank. In fact, banks are the standard lending resources for business. Statistically, banks are the largest single source for loans and financing. Obviously, a bank depends on loans and the interest earned for a major source of its revenue. Banks are in the money business and should certainly be thought of when you need money for start-up or expansion capital. Willie Sutton was no dummy. He knew where to go for money and so should you.

Some banks have even initiated specialized programs designed to attract start-up and other newer companies as customers. Bank of America recently opened its first operation in Washington, D.C., many miles from its base in San Francisco. This branch, known as the Bank of America Community Development Bank (CDB), is not really a bank but rather a resource for lending to small businesses.[3]

A bank bases the amount of interest it charges on two factors: the relative size and financial history of the borrower and the risk the bank will take in providing the loan. Remember, by risk here we mean not the real risk, but rather the bank's perception of the risk. You may be certain that its money is safe and

---

[3] Bank of America has CDB loans out in twelve states (at this writing more than one billion dollars) and is actively seeking opportunities in small businesses (especially minority- and woman-owned). For additional infromation on this program, contact your local Bank of America branch or the CDB headquarters in Walnut Creek, CA.

secure in the hands of you and your business, but it is the bank's perception that counts.

In order to have some idea of what to expect in the area of interest, you should understand something about the prime rate. Interest charges by the bank are always based on some factor of the prime interest rate. The prime (meaning the first) interest rate for each bank is the lowest rate banks charge their most favored customers—are usually large companies and organizations with an extensive history with the bank or rock-solid financial attributes.

As to your home business needs, keep in mind that banks charge smaller and riskier customers an interest rate some number above the prime rate. As noted above, the risk aspect is the bank's perception, not yours.

A final note on interest. Some bankers have told us that there may be some flexibility as to interest rate. The bank will say that it doesn't fluctuate from its loan guidelines (and this probably is quite true regarding the larger institutions), but smaller regional or local banks may negotiate their interest rate under all circumstances. As noted in the discussion of bank limitations above, you can negotiate. At least, give it a try.

Savings and Loan Organizations

The differences between savings and loan associations and commercial banks are narrowing as each receive permission to conduct more activities in the former domain of the other. Savings and loans became famous (or one might say infamous) after the savings and loan bailout by the federal government, but they are still around and even Willie Sutton would agree they too have money. Thus, do not forego them as a potential traditional lending resource. While the savings and loans may have been formed under a different type of charter and were originally established to facilitate the lending of money for home mortgages, they have gradually evolved into most full-service banking operations.

You should be aware that savings and loans have some government (both federal and state) restrictions on where and how they can operate as compared to commercial banks. Their financial goals and motivations are similar to a commercial bank. They lend money and charge for loans based on the prime rate of interest or some variation of it.

It doesn't take a rocket scientist to figure that because of the 1991–92 savings and loan debacle, which resulted in the demise of many institutions (both large and small), the remaining savings and loans are taking a very careful look at any business loan application. You can expect that a savings and loan will probably now require that any loan be backed up by an equivalent amount of collateral.

Loan Companies

Loan companies are private organizations in the business of lending money and making money doing it. These entities exist in most United States cities and communities and are a plentiful source of funding. However, unlike banks, which obtain funds from many different sources, loan companies have to rely upon their own capital for raising money. The result to you will be, in all likelihood, a higher interest rate than that available through a bank or savings and loan. In some instances, they can be a number of points above the prime rate. The loan company may also charge additional fees for loan origination. These fees are usually "points," meaning a percentage of the loan sought—i.e., three points would be three percent of the principal loan amount.

Loan companies are considered collateral lenders because they rely heavily upon the borrower's ability to back up the loan fully with a pledge or assignment of assets. So, while it is possible to obtain a loan upon the mere signature (i.e., unsecured) from a bank, it is not likely that would ever happen through a loan company.

Because loan companies are private firms and are not under the same scrutiny as banks and savings and loans, they can have disparate operating and lending policies. This can result in a wide variation in their interest rates. Thus, if you are thinking of borrowing from a loan company, shop around before you settle on a particular lender. For a listing of loan companies in your area, check your classified directory. Most accountants and lawyers who deal with commercial transactions would know the names of the more reliable loan companies. As with any other legal transaction, be careful with whom you deal.

A good caveat is in order here that applies to all money sources: Know thy lender. A number of politicians and others can tell horror stories about borrowing money or getting financially involved with the wrong people. Not to frighten you or to detract from the many perfectly legitimate private loan companies around, we want to alert you to vigilance regarding borrowing money from private sources. None of us wants to go for a swim wearing a concrete bathing suit.

Insurance Companies, Pension Funds and Unions

Larger existing businesses may be able to tap these three sources of money for direct loans or for investment purposes. These three potential financing resources have one thing in common: they are generally interested only in making loans of substantial size to the highest rated firms. Thus, they would probably not be interested in making loans to start-up or even "going" smaller businesses. We have mentioned them here for your home business because you might just convince a pension fund manager, or beneficiary of a retirement plan or small union to participate with you in the business. Be aware that insurance companies, pension and retirement funds and unions each have restricted guidelines for their investment or financial participation.

Credit Unions

Another significant, and sometimes overlooked, source of funding is credit unions. Credit unions were originally established with two objectives: to provide a savings vehicle for members and to lend to members in need of loans, primarily for automobile and appliance purchases, or for emergency financial needs.

More recently, credit unions have expanded their lending operations to include nonmembers and even to participating in loans outside of traditional financial investments. In the past, credit unions would put their funds only in United States Treasury Bills and notes, certificates of deposit and highly rated corporate bonds. Now they are more aggressive and seek out other investments, even direct company loans (including on occasion new start-ups), where they can realize a much higher rate of return or actually secure an equity interest in the company to which they are making the loan.

Small Business Investment Companies

These are privately owned companies licensed and insured by the United States Small Business Administration. Their reason for being is to provide capital to smaller firms. Small Business Investment Companies usually focus on the specific field or industry where the principals have a background or special interest. These include such areas as high technology firms, or agricultural, manufacturing or real estate companies.

Several Small Business Investment Companies exist in each state. In order to find them, contact the nearest Office of the Small Business Administration, (a listing of all SBA offices is contained in Appendix B) or obtain a listing of them for your area from the United States Department of Commerce or your local congressional representative.

Private Investors

We all know that certain individuals or groups of individuals make investments and loans, usually in exchange for an equity interest in a company. These people may operate as private individuals or as a group of like-minded souls (who usually rate the title venture capitalists—see next category below). Private investors may become involved financially with existing concerns and new business start-ups. Obviously, investor objectives and goals vary as widely as the personalities of the individuals. There can be no discounting the importance, however, of the individual investor to business financing.

Most private investors are looking for the value in their investment as an end in itself. They normally want no part of the day-to-day activities of the company, nor are they interested in becoming involved with ongoing business decisions. Some investors will limit the types of business they will invest in or the amount they will place at risk. Investors can participate in a business through either a private placement or public offering of shares. We will discuss the legal implications further in Chapter 7.

Finding a private investor who takes interest in your home business is the challenge. Often local bankers, accountants, lawyers or your local newspaper's Sunday classified advertising pages can help.

Venture Capitalists

One might refer to the private investor above as an amateur. The venture capitalist, on the other hand, is a professional. This individual or group almost always provides funding for an equity or ownership interest in the firm and rarely lends money, although some combination deals are possible such as a loan convertible to equity. The sophisticated venture capitalist has a background or knowledge in the field of interest and is usually interested only in start-up or plateau (second round) financing of businesses in that field.

Venture capitalists usually will not take an active role in the management of everyday affairs of the company for which they are providing funds; however, in order to protect or oversee their funds they may want to join the company's board of directors themselves or nominate a designee to sit on the board as their eyes and ears.

The field of venture capital financing has become quite a big business in recent years. Large-scale business success by founders of now-large companies and possible golden handshakes or buy-outs may have also led to the rise in people who seek to invest in (and occasionally participate in) the right new business for them. Finding these people has always been a challenge but it is not impossible.

A number of books, directories and even software programs list principal firms and venture capital resources. We list several of these in Appendix C. Investment firms are even available on the Internet (e.g., Accel Partners at http://www.accel.com and Olympic Venture Partners at http://product.com/Olympic). A good up-to-date directory of the World Wide Web can lead to more contacts, as can your local banker, commercial attorney or accountant.

Many areas of the United States have venture groups. For example, when he was practicing law, Charles was a member of the Connecticut Venture Group. These organizations usually have fairly open membership and allow members (and sometimes guests) to discuss their deals briefly at "one-minute forums" of regular meetings. The membership rosters of such groups might lead to very good contacts.

Let's also not forget that most major and even some minor brokerage houses or investment firms have venture capital and/or underwriting departments or groups. They are always looking for the "right deal."

NONTRADITIONAL FUNDING SOURCES

Nontraditional money sources are limited only by your imagination and creativity.

We supply a few suggestions. You should use these merely as ideas to stimulate your own thinking about other places or ways to raise funds.

Customers and Clients

In truth, if your business, practice or idea is a good one and people with whom you have worked have had a good experience, they might be interested in participating financially. Thus clients, customers or potential customers can be an excellent source of funding.

If you came up with a wonderful idea and could show a potential customer how it could benefit his or her business, isn't it logical to think that he or she would invest or lend money to you? In our field of dispute resolution, one major firm is funded by a consortium of insurance companies who felt it was cheaper to support the success of an alternative dispute resolution firm than to pay attorneys' fees and court costs in all cases.

We heard about a woman who wanted to open a travel agency in her home. She contacted a large company near her that agreed to fund a considerable piece of the start-up in exchange for special considerations such as ticket delivery and discounted travel when possible.

A caveat: Watch the ethics of the situation. Many of you will practice or do business in fields that have strong ethical codes against self-dealing. Others of you will be troubled by a moral sense of what is right or wrong. As Charles says in *Ethics for Government Employees*: if it doesn't feel right, don't do it.[4]

Suppliers

Like customers or potential customers, suppliers can be a great source of funding. Let's face it, if they can see a major market for them coming out of your success, why wouldn't they want to help you?

Suppliers will often provide and finance specialized equipment that is necessary for use with the products they provide. A classic example is food wholesalers who will often provide display cases, shelving and other equipment. They get the recognition, you get the equipment and you buy additional needs from them.

We also know of a software developer of considerable talent who works from his home. The money to set up his original computer system came from a software firm that gladly supplied the equipment in exchange for a right of first refusal on all of his new programs. Note how these relationships represent win-win deals!

Leasing Companies

Traditionally, leasing companies and organizations mainly provided motor vehicles and other large fixed assets. Gradually, this role has changed. In recent yeas, these same leasing companies have diversified their operations and are now known to pay for the purchase of new inventory and provide money for leasehold improvements such as decorating and remodeling. They may even provide money for working capital. Because leasing companies derive their income from the use of capital, many have recently moved into areas previously considered the domain of banks and loan companies.

---

[4] Crisp also publishes a very worthy book on business ethics, *Ethics in Business,* by Robert and Dorothy Maddux.

Local Economic Development Companies

These organizations have been formed in a geographical or market area to attract new business to that place. Frequently established in rural communities and small towns, they often consist of local banks, real estate firms, and business leaders who band together to bring in new industry. These nonprofit institutions may be in a position to offer land and buildings and even capital. Certainly, they know the pulse of the area and where you may be able to find local financial support. This is especially true if your business (albeit based in the home) will create local jobs, directly or indirectly. Local economic development companies often obtain their funds very creatively. Sometimes, the county or the state will also offer support to the local company or agency.

Advertise for Money

Many entrepreneurs find that they can stimulate interest on the part of lenders or investors by running a display advertisement in the business section or under the appropriate heading (such as "Investor Wanted," "Capital Needed" or "Business Opportunity") in the classified section of your local newspaper. The instances where we know that this has been done have, quite frankly, yielded few positive results. Many of the respondents wanted to sell something themselves, usually a product or service.

We are told classified advertising for capital can be done successfully. If you do not have a problem with confidentiality of your project or yourself, it might be easy for you to try this approach. Keep in mind that this could mean inviting ad respondents to your home. If you decide the advertisement is a good idea, carefully choose the publication. For example, in our home area (approximately seventy miles west of Washington, D.C.), an advertisement in *The Washington Post* would probably yield better results than in our weekly newspaper.

In the ad itself, it is probably a good idea to specify the amount of money needed and the type of business for which you will use it. We are firm believers in honesty up front. If someone is interested, let them know as much as possible to avoid surprises or disappointments later. Initially you can maintain confidentiality for both parties through the use of a post office box or newspaper box number, but eventually you will make direct contact if the interest is serious.

We offer below a sample advertisement you might use as your starting point:

Capital Needed: Start-up home business in burgeoning network marketing field offering excellent food-supplement products needs investor-partner. $50K buys half interest. Potential profit is $75K per year. Contact Ed Johnson, EJ Health Foods, 555-1234.

ON YOUR OWN

As stated earlier, nontraditional sources for funding can be quite surprising. Using the form below, see if you can generate possibilities for your own home business other than those suggested above:

Potential Source	Contact Person/Phone	Why They Should Invest
1.		
2.		
3.		
4.		
5.		
6.		

A number of good books are available to assist in finding money and in generating innovative ideas about how to raise funds. We list some in Appendix C.

GOVERNMENT PROGRAMS

Readers from most countries may be able to call upon government program(s) ranging from direct financial subsidy to incentive awards.

Many programs are available through Departments or Ministries of Commerce, Business, Trade and/or Industry. In the United States, a number of programs are available at both the state and federal level. Before discussing any of these, we must remind you that governments are financially pressed themselves, both in the United States and elsewhere. With new emphasis on cost-cutting, less government and more self-reliance by citizens, it is very possible that some of the resources listed in this section may be reduced or even eliminated.

At this writing, the United States Congress and President are at loggerheads over what will happen next with the federal budget and the annual deficits. In spite of this, most observers agree that stimulation of business is a positive thing for the economy. It is probably fair to suggest that government assistance, rather than support, will be the trend for the balance of this century.

Some programs are certain to survive the legislative scalpel, even though their parent organizations or administrative structures may face reorganization. Among expected survivors are the Small Business Administration and some, if not all, SBA programs. As we have heard now for several years in the United States, government cannot be a crutch. Potential entrepreneurs should prepare to arrange financial resources on their own. However, government can be a coach and educator.

In calling upon government (either the programs we cite here, their successors, or others), readers will have to be both sensitive and alert to the possibility that a program could be altered or even canceled at any time. Projects under application, but not yet approved, could suffer.

In dealing with any agencies or organizations that rely on these government programs for funding or guarantees, be certain to check in advance as to its viability and the stability of funding. As you will see, many programs require extensive paperwork and back-up documentation. It would be a shame to engage in a lengthy and expensive preparation process only to find out the agency no longer exists, or the program exists but is not funded.

Now that we covered the bleak realism, let's recapture some optimism and look at some of the currently existing programs and government small business schemes. The information contained in this section has been obtained directly from SBA informational sources.

In the United States, the best-known federal government agency for small business assistance is the Small Business Administration. In addition to the SBA, the Service Corps of Retired Executive (SCORE) and the Small Business Development Centers (SBDCs), mentioned briefly above, help small businesses with financial planning, business counseling, and act as special advocates on a variety of small business topics.

If you are seeking governmental counseling, the nearest SCORE or SBDC office can schedule an appointment with a counselor. These counselors have a broad range of business expertise and a great willingness to help small businesses. They also work closely with the SBA to provide information and advice.

SBA Standard 7(a) Guarantee Program

If you are interested in obtaining a standard SBA loan, the SBA advises you to see your own banker. Be certain to take with you the information listed below:

- Cash flow projection

- Personal financial statements

- Personal résumé of expertise

- List of what the money is to be used for (inventory, working capital, etc.)

- If you have an existing business or are buying a business, financial statements for the past three (3) years and the current year-to-date should be provided.

If the bank you talk to is interested in making an SBA-guaranteed loan it will provide an application package for the SBA loan. Follow the instructions and return the completed package to the bank. The banker will send the completed application to the SBA. You and the bank negotiate the interest rate and loan terms. If the SBA approves the loan, the bank will advance the money and you will repay the bank according to the negotiated loan terms just as you would a non-SBA loan.

It should be noted that the SBA does not have direct loan funds in any category. Therefore, you should give your best effort to obtain a loan from your banker in cooperation with SBA.

In addition to the standard SBA loan program (technically referred to as the "7(a) loan guarantee"), there is a new program designed for smaller amounts and easier application process.

The SBA LowDoc Program

Because of the relative ease of application and potential for widespread use in financing home businesses, we'll discuss the new program in some detail. The program is called the SBA LowDoc Program. According to the SBA, it makes applying for an SBA Loan guarantee more user-friendly than it's ever been. Combining a greatly simplified application process with a rapid response from SBA loan officers—usually only two or three days—LowDoc slashes pages and pages of bureaucracy and red tape out of the loan process.

In the SBA's own words: "Creativity and good common sense has produced a program that will put loans into the hands of thousands of credit-worthy entrepreneurs to start or expand their businesses, create jobs and enrich the economic vitality of their communities."

SBA's LowDoc, or low documentation, loan program is a response to past complaints that SBA's loan application process for smaller loans was needlessly cumbersome for both borrowers and lenders that participate in SBA's 7(a) General Business Loan Guarantee Program.

Any small business eligible under the regular 7(a) loan program can apply under LowDoc if its average annual sales for the previous three years are $5,000,000 or less and it employees 100 or fewer individuals, including the owner, partners, or principals. Most home businesses we know of would fit into this category.

LowDoc streamlines the loan application process for guaranteed loans up to $100,000. SBA reports that the approval process focuses on character, credit and business experience. LowDoc was developed with input and help from both small business owners and commercial lenders. Under LowDoc, the SBA can guarantee up to 80% of a loan made by a commercial lender to an existing business, a business purchaser, or a business start-up.

LowDoc relies heavily on a lender's experience and judgment of a borrower's credit history and character. The primary considerations are the borrower's willingness and ability to repay debts, as shown by his or her personal and business credit history, and by past projected business cash flow. No predetermined percentage of equity is required and lack of full collateral is not a determining factor. However, the SBA alerts that all available collateral will be taken.

The application form for loans less than $50,000 consists of a single page. Applications for loans from $50,001 to $100,000 include the short form application plus the applicant's income tax returns for the previous three years, personal financial statements and credit reports for all other guarantors and coworkers of the business. Commercial lenders will probably require additional paperwork to satisfy their own requirements. Legislation, regulation, and executive orders may require other documentation. These are dealt with at the loan closing.

As with 7(a) loans, borrowers and lenders negotiate interest rates, generally setting them at market rates. They are subject to SBA maximums of 2.25 points above the prime rate for loans of less than seven years' maturity and up to 2.75 points above the prime rate for loans of seven years or longer. For loans less than $25,000, lenders may add an additional percentage to the above rates. For loans between $25,001 and $50,000, lenders may add and additional 1%. The guarantee fee will be based on the guaranteed portion of the loan at 2%.

Borrowers can use LowDoc loan proceeds for most legitimate business purposes, including working capital and expanding, renovating or purchasing a business, machinery and equipment, or inventory. Loan proceeds cannot be used for distribution to owners or principals or for payment of personal debt. Applications for purchasing an existing business must include a copy of the terms of sale, financial statements on the existing business, statement on the benefits the business receives as a result of the change of ownership, and a statement as to the relationship between the buyer and the seller.

Additional information on regular SBA 7(a) and LowDoc programs are available from the SBA regional offices listed in Appendix B. Lending institutions who routinely provide SBA guaranteed loans are also good sources for information and application materials. A number of state and private firms also work closely with the SBA in providing information, contact names and counsel as to SBA programs. The regional SBA office or your state development agency can direct you to these resources.

The information for this section and the application form in the Appendix were provided by the SBA in November 1995. Be certain to check with the SBA or participating lenders for any informational changes and/or updates. In addition to the information contained in this section, a number of very good resources outside of the SBA exist to assist you in understanding how SBA programs operate and how best to participate in them. Perhaps the best place to go for information is a participating financial institution. A list of such banks is available from the SBA and is contained in Orlando Antonini's excellent book *Getting A Business Loan* (available from Crisp Publications). In addition to a step-by-step guide to SBA and other conventional loan programs, Antonini lists the banks in the SBA Certified Lender and Preferred Lender programs by state.

A FINAL NOTE ON FUNDRAISING

Obviously in a few pages of one small book we could not possibly cover every aspect of finding money and list every resource. We've tried to direct you to some good places and to provide you with the context in which the quest for funding should be undertaken. As noted above, we suggest you be creative and participate actively in finding new and as yet untested sources. This might take the form of a local union's extra funds (with which it is willing to take some risks), a local cooperative whereby several people get together to pool resources and financial targets, or a foreign contact who wants to get involved in a business in your area.

The point is: if you are going to beat the odds (remember the frightening statistics from the introduction about business failures) and make a success of your business, you must demonstrate some creativity and initiative. Raising money may be the best place to start this.

And if by chance you should not succeed in your first step of raising money, don't give up. The late Colonel Sanders (of Kentucky Fried Chicken fame) was turned down dozens of times before he found a financial backer. He knew his concept had merit, he had the commitment and tenaciousness needed to launch a new business and, most of all, he proved he was right! You can too.

INTRODUCTION TO BORROWING

The first part of this chapter presented several potential sources of financing. Now it's time to discuss how to approach these sources and convince them to lend you the money you need to start or expand your home business.

All too many small business persons, including principals of home businesses, have difficulty getting a traditional lending institution to advance them money for their business. A minority of others have no trouble raising funds, but are surprised to find what they would consider onerous preconditions imposed on their loans. Many entrepreneurs fail to realize that banks and other lenders operate under certain principles and policies, some of which are variable and others of which are not.

Inexperience with borrowing procedures often creates resentment and bitterness by persons seeking financial assistance. Knowledge of the financial facts of business life (i.e., the reality of looking for funding) can save embarrassment or disappointment. Even more important, such information can help you borrow money at a time when your businesses really needs it.

Let's look now at the factors the SBA recommends for consideration by institutions in its lending and guarantee programs, which include: (1) creditworthiness of the borrower, (2) kinds of loans, (3) amount of money needed, (4) collateral, (5) loan restrictions and limitations, (6) the loan application, and (7) standards that the lender uses to evaluate the application. Later in the chapter we will discuss equity and other capital resources.

Is the Firm Creditworthy?

The ability to obtain money when you need it is as necessary to the operation of your business as a good location, the right equipment, reliable sources of supplies and materials, and an adequate labor force. Before a bank or any other lending agency will lend you money, the loan officer must feel satisfied with the answers to the five following questions.

What sort of person are you, the prospective borrower? By all odds, the character of the borrower comes first. Next is your ability to manage your business. No bones about it, these are personal issues and you must be prepared to deal with this kind of inquiry. Thus, for example, if you had a personal bankruptcy or other credit problem in the past, have a good explanation and possible alternative comfort (such as a cosigner) for the lender when the issue comes up.

What are you going to do with the money? The answer to this question will determine the type of loan that the lender might approve—i.e., short- or long-term. For example, money used to purchase seasonal inventory will require quicker repayment than money used to buy fixed assets.

When and how do you plan to pay it back? You banker's judgment of your own integrity and business ability and the type of loan being sought will decide the answer to this question.

Is the cushion in the loan large enough? In other words, does the amount requested make suitable allowance for unexpected developments? The banker (who probably knows a lot less about your business than you do) decides this question on the basis of your financial statement, which should set forth the condition of your business, and on the collateral pledge.

What is the outlook for business in general, and for your business in particular? Adequate financial data is a must. Let's face it, if the economy is down or there is a glut of businesses in your field, you can expect your banker to be far more resistant than if you approached him or her when business is booming in general and in your field the sky's the limit.

The banker wants to make loans to solvent, profitable and growing businesses. The two basic financial statements used to determine those conditions are the balance sheet and profit-and-loss statement. The former is the major yardstick for solvency and the latter for profits. A continuous series of these two statements over a period of time is the principal device for measuring financial stability and growth potential. (For a discussion of essential financial statements, see Chapter 3.)

In interviewing loan applicants and in studying their records, the banker is especially interested in the following facts and figures:

General Information

- Are the books and records up-to-date and in good condition?

- Have they been prepared by the company or an independent auditor or accountant?

- Have standard accounting practices and principles been used?

- What is the condition of accounts payable? Of notes payable?

- What are the salaries of the principals and other key players?

- Are all taxes being paid currently or are there unpaid taxes?

- What is the order backlog?

- What is the number of employees?

- What is the business's insurance coverage?

Accounts Receivable

- Have some of the accounts receivable already been pledged to another creditor?

- What is the accounts receivable turnover?

- What is the receivables aging situation, that is, is the accounts receivable total weakened because many customers are too far behind in their payments?

- Has a sufficient reserve been set up to cover doubtful accounts?

- How much do the large accounts owe and what percentage of your total accounts does this amount represent?

Inventories

- Is merchandise in readily saleable condition or will it have to be marked down?
- How much raw material is on hand?
- How much work is in process?
- How much of the inventory is finished goods?
- Is there any obsolete inventory?
- Has an excessive amount of inventory been consigned to customers?
- Is inventory turnover in line with the turnover for other businesses in the same industry—i.e., is money being tied up too long in inventory?

Fixed Assets

- What kind of fixed assets does the business use (or own)?
- What is the type, age and condition of the businesses equipment?
- What are the depreciation policies?
- What are the details of mortgages or conditional sales contracts?
- What are the future acquisition or update plans for the equipment?

What Kind of Money Do You Need?

When you set out to borrow money for your firm, it is important to know the kind of money you need from a bank or other lending institution. For purposes of this discussion, we refer to the three main kinds of money: short-term loan funds, term borrowing and equity capital.

The purpose for which the funds will be used is an important factor in deciding the kind of money needed. But even so, deciding what kind of money to use is not always easy. It is sometimes complicated by the fact that you may be using some of the various kinds of money at the same time and even, on occasion, for what seems to be the same purposes.

Also, keep in mind that a very important distinguishing factor in the types of money is the source of repayment. Generally, short-term loans are repaid from the liquidation of current assets, the purchase of which the loan money financed. Long-term loans are usually paid from earnings.

Short-Term Bank Loans

You can use short-term bank loans for purposes such as financing accounts receivable, for say thirty to sixty days. Or you can use them for purposes that take longer to pay off, such as for building a seasonal inventory over a period of five to six months. Usually lenders expect short-term loans to be repaid after their purposes have been served. For example, accounts receivable loans are repaid when the outstanding accounts have been paid by the borrower's customers, and inventory loans are repaid when the inventory has been converted into saleable merchandise.

Banks grant such money on your general credit reputation with an unsecured loan or a secured loan. The unsecured loan is the most frequently used form of bank credit for short-term purposes. You do not have to put up collateral because the bank relies on your credit reputation.

Term Borrowing

Term borrowing provides funds which are repayable over a period of considerable time. Term borrowing can be broken down into two forms: (1) intermediate—loans longer than one year but less than five years, and (2) long-term—loans for more than five years. Be aware, however, that a financial professional will likely consider as a long-term debt any money due to the repaid in longer than one year.

At this point, for your purpose of matching the kind of money to the needs of your home business, think of term borrowing as a loan that you will probably pay back in periodic installments from earnings.

Equity Capital

Some people confuse term borrowing with equity (or investment) capital. However, there is a big difference. As you will learn later in this chapter, you don't have to repay equity money. It is money you get by selling a part interest in your business.

We will discuss equity fund-raising a little later in more detail.

How Much Money Do You Reasonably Require?

The amount of money you need to borrow (raise) depends on the purpose for which you needs funds. Figuring out the amount of money required for business construction, conversion, or expansion—term loans or equity capital—is relatively easy. Suppliers, vendors and equipment manufacturers, architects, and builders will readily supply you with cost estimates. On the other hand, the amount of working capital you need depends upon the type of business you're conducting and good practice for that business in terms of both ready and back-up capital. In previous chapters we discussed the need for adequate planning. Here we consider in some detail the financial institution's considerations about your plan and budget.

Rule-of-thumb ratios for working capital are available for many fields. Some home businesses will involve a franchiser, upline person or other mentor who will guide you as to what you should need. These guidelines may be helpful as a starting point; however, they will not be running your business—you will. Therefore, in the end *you* must make a determination as to what is a sufficient amount to have on hand or available through a financing source. A detailed projection of sources and uses of funds over some future period of time—usually for 12 months—will provide far more reliable financial needs data than someone else's guidance. This kind of projection is developed through the combination of a predicted budget and a cash forecast.

The budget is based on recent operating experience plus your own best judgment of performance during the coming period. The cash forecast is your estimate of cash receipts and disbursements during the budget period. The budget and cash forecast together represent your plan for meeting the working capital requirements of your home business.

To plan your working capital requirements, you must know as much as you can about the cash flow you expect your business to generate. This financial intelligence involves a reasoned consideration of all elements of cash receipts and disbursements at the time they occur. These critical elements to your financial intelligence are listed on the profit-and-loss statement, which should be modified to show cash flow. When these elements are realistically estimated based on the best available data, they should be projected for each month needed to repay your loan or supply a return on investment (ROI) to an equity investor.

What Kind of Collateral is Available and/or Needed?

In the best of all worlds, your signature is the only security the bank needs when making a loan. At most other times (some cynics would argue all the time), the bank requires additional assurance that the money they supply can and will be repaid. This assurance varies according to the bank's policies and governing regulations and the basic philosophy (liberal or conservative) of its principals. Thus, the kind and amount of security depends on both the bank and the borrower's situation.

If the borrower's financial statements alone cannot justify the loan required, a pledge of security may bridge the gap. The standard types of bank security arrangements or assets that can be collateralized are:

- Endorsers, comakers and guarantors
- Assignment of leases
- Warehouse receipts
- Trust receipts and floor planning
- Chattel mortgages
- Real estate
- Accounts receivable
- Cash such as savings accounts
- Life insurance policies with cash value
- Stocks and bonds

In the majority of states where the Uniform Commercial Code (UCC) has been enacted, it will govern the documentary requirements for the collateral transaction. While it may not feel that way to the borrower, in truth, the UCC has greatly simplified the paperwork for recording loan transactions. The UCC also acts as the bulletin board that alerts other people to the transaction in question and to the fact that the collateral is now burdened or encumbered by the debt obligation underlying it.

Endorsers, Comakers, and Guarantors

It is not at all uncommon for borrowers to get some other person or people to sign a note in order to beef up the credit of the principal borrower. Endorsing the loan documents obliges the second person or persons to be responsible for the debt if the primary person does not or cannot pay the money back. These endorsers are contingently liable for the note they sign. If the borrower fails to pay up, the bank expects the endorsers to make the note good. Some banks will even ask the endorser to pledge assets or securities.

A comaker is one who creates an obligation jointly with the borrower. The comaker in essence stands in the shoes of the primary borrower. Thus, in the event of default, the bank has the choice of collecting directly from either the maker or the comaker.

A guarantor is one who guarantees the payment of a note by signing a guaranty commitment. These documents are independent of (but obviously related to) the loan agreement or note. Government lenders and many private institutional lenders (as contrasted to individual lenders) often require guarantees from officers or corporations in order to assure continuity of the management of the business who qualified for the loan. Sometimes a manufacturer or major supplier will act as a guarantor for customers.

Assignment of Leases

The assigned lease as security is similar to the guarantee. If requires a separate document of assignment. It has been used in some franchise situations. Here's how it works: The bank lends the money on a building and takes a mortgage. Then the lease, which the dealer and the parent franchise company work out, is assigned to the bank so that it automatically receives the rent payments that guarantee repayment of the loan.

Warehouse Receipts

Banks also take commodities as security by lending money on a warehouse receipt. Such a receipt is usually delivered directly to the bank and shows that the merchandise used as security either has been placed in a public warehouse or has been left on the business premises under the control of one of the business's employees who is bonded (as in field warehousing). Such loans are generally made on staple or standard merchandise that can be readily marketed. The typical warehouse receipt loan is for a percentage of the estimated value of the goods used as security.

It is not too likely these will be seen as collateral factors in most home businesses.

Trust Receipts and Floor Planning

Certain merchandise, such as automobiles, appliances, and boats, must be displayed to be sold. These sales are usually conducted through retail sales outlets, which are rarely home businesses. Applicability of this type of collateral arrangement is improbable in your business, but we feel you should know something about it anyway. The way many smaller sellers of expensive merchandise can afford such displays is by borrowing money. Such loans are often secured by a note and a trust receipt.

This so-called trust receipt constitutes the legal backup for the concept you've probably heard called "floor planning." It is used for serial-numbered merchandise. The floor plan system works as follows: when the merchandise is received the trust receipt is signed, the borrower agrees to keep the merchandise in trust for the bank, and promises to pay the bank (in whole or part as agreed with the bank) as the goods are sold "from the floor."

Chattel Mortgages

A well-accepted method for buying business equipment is to obtain the money from the bank, buying the equipment and giving the bank a lien on the equipment you are buying and even other physical property if required.

Receipt of goods to become collateral by chattel mortgage is not automatic. The amount of collateral to be allowed via chattel mortgage is up to the bank. It will evaluate both the present and future market value of the equipment being used to secure the loan and decide either how much to lend or how much merchandise, equipment or other "chattel" your business needs to mortgage to secure the underlying debt. The lender will also consider how rapidly the chattel will depreciate. Does the borrower have the necessary fire, theft, property damage, and public liability insurance on the equipment? Obviously since the lender has a property interest in the goods by mortgage, it has to be sure that the borrower protects the equipment.

Real Estate

Real estate is another form of collateral for long-term loans. In many ways, it is among the best collateral categories available. When taking a real estate mortgage, the bank finds out: (1) the location of the real estate, (2) its physical condition, (3) its foreclosure value, and (4) the amount of insurance carried on the property.

Accounts Receivable

Many banks and other lenders such as factors lend money on accounts receivable. The business is thus asking its clients or customers to pay the note.

The lender may take accounts receivable on a notification or a non-notification plan. Under the notification plan, the lender informs the purchaser of the goods that his or her account has been assigned to it, and asks the purchaser to pay the lender directly. Under the non-notification plan, the borrower's customers continue to pay the business the sums due on their accounts and the business pays the lender as it collects the money.

Cash or Savings Accounts

It has been said that the best borrower is the one who doesn't need the money. This paradoxical statement may sound humorous, but often lenders seek absolute assurance that the monies will be repaid. The most liquid asset is money itself. Therefore, the lender may ask for cash, which it will hold as security, or a savings account passbook as collateral.

Secured credit cards are a form of collateralized lending. The borrower opens a savings account and the bank allows use of a credit card up to an agreed limit (usually the amount of the savings balance or more as agreed).

Life Insurance

Banks will sometimes lend up to the entire cash value of a life insurance policy. You have to assign the policy to the bank.

If the policy is on the life of an executive of a small corporation, corporate resolutions must be made authorizing the assignment. Most insurance companies allow you to sign the policy back to the original beneficiary when the assignment to the bank ends. Be certain to check with your insurance company before offering the policy cash value as collateral. The company may have some conditions or terms you must comply with before they'll assign the cash value to someone other than you.

Some people like to use life insurance as collateral rather than borrow directly from insurance companies. One reason is that a bank loan is often more convenient to obtain and usually may be obtained at a lower interest rate.

Obviously, if the debt defaults, the bank takes the cash value, which will probably diminish the amount payable at the time of death. This potential to affect beneficiaries should be considered by those thinking of using a life insurance policy as collateral.

Stocks and Bonds

Stocks and bonds also make very acceptable collateral; however, they must be marketable. As a protection against market declines and possible expenses of liquidation, banks usually lend no more than a percentage of the market value of high grade stock (usually not more than 75% at a fixed date). On federal government or high grade municipal bonds, they may be willing to lend 90% or more of their market value.

Because these are readily marketable securities, the bank may ask the borrower for additional security of payment whenever the market value of the stocks or bonds drops below the bank's required margin.

The Lender's Rules

Lending institutions are not just interested in loan repayments. They want borrowers with healthy profit-making businesses and long-term relationships with growing customers. Therefore, whether or not collateral is required for a loan, lenders will probably set loan limitations and restrictions (i.e., Lender's Rules) to protect themselves against unnecessary risk and at the same time against poor management practices by their borrowers. Often some owner-managers consider loan limitations a burden. Home business people who are used to or who crave the freedom to march to their own drummer may have problems with this. Other borrowers feel that reasonable limitations also offer an opportunity for improving their management techniques. Some even appreciate the discipline imposed by the lender in tight-fisted money management.

With regard to longer term loans, both lender and borrower must consider:

1. The net earning power of the borrowing business,

2. The capability of borrower personnel to run the business,

3. The long range success prospects of the business, and

4. The long range outlook for the industry of which the borrower is a part.

Lender adjustments for these factors can limit on the flexibility of the company to manage its own destiny and can increase as the duration of the loan extends.

Limitations That May be Imposed

The types of limitations or restrictions that may be imposed depend on the business undertaken and the field in general. If the company is a good risk with solid performance, good management, a growing market and super financial controls, minimal limitations will be set. A poor loan risk, or course, is different; the limitations will be greater and there will be less operating freedom.

Let's look now at the kinds of limitations and restrictions which the lender may set. Knowing what they are can help you decide where to look for money and what you are able to sacrifice for it.

While we've said above that each lender operates within its own guidelines (always complying with legal requirements such as margins), there are some "standard" limitations which you will often find when you borrow money. They are

1. Repayment terms

2. Pledging or use of security

3. Periodic reporting

A loan agreement, as you may already know, is a custom-made legal document covering, or referring to, all the terms and conditions of the loan. In fact, it should contain all the terms, and verbal (parol) modifications will not usually amend it. Through use of this agreement, the lender accomplishes two critical things. First, it protects its position as a creditor (keeps that position in as protected a state as it was on the date the loan was made). Second, it assures repayment according to the terms.

The lender grants the loan on the premise that the borrower's business should generate enough funds to repay the loan while taking care of other needs. The lender considers that cash inflow should be great enough to do this without hurting the working capital of the borrower.

The actual restrictions or legal limitations in a loan agreement come under a section of the document known as covenants. Negative covenants are things that the borrower may not do without prior approval from the lender. Some examples of negative covenants are further additions to the borrower's total assignment to others of the borrower's assets, and issuance of dividends in excess of the terms of the loan agreement.

Positive covenants spell out things that the borrower must do. Some fairly standard examples of these are maintenance of a minimum net working capital, carrying of adequate insurance, repaying the loan according to the terms of the agreement, and supplying the lender with regular and periodic financial statements and reports.

In spite of the parol evidence rule, which prohibits verbal modification of most agreements in writing, loan agreements may be amended from time to time and exceptions made. Certain provisions may be waived from one year to the next with the consent of the lender and in compliance with the document's own provisions for modification and amendment. Don't assume that because the bank is big and you are little you, you have no say in the terms of the loan. **You can negotiate!**

Remember, when you go to borrow money, be prepared to deal with all the lender's issues or conditions, but don't be shy about having a few of your own. As Alarid says, "thrash out the lending terms before you sign. It is good practice no matter how badly you may need the money. Ask to see the papers in advance of the loan closing. Legitimate lenders are glad to cooperate."

You will probably want to have your attorney review the loan agreement. Be sure he or she is familiar with commercial transactions and credit arrangements. Not all attorneys are informed on all topics. The lawyer who helped you at the closing for the home where your business is located may not be the best choice to review the loan documents for the business. There is no question that you can negotiate with the lender; but once the terms have been agreed upon and the loan is made (or authorized, as in the case of SBA loan guarantee arrangement), you are bound by them.

THE LOAN APPLICATION

O.K. We now have a better sense of what the lenders are looking for and how they will look at the deal. It's time to think about the actual application process itself.

Every bank and other private lending institution, as well as the Small Business Administration, require a loan application on which you may be required to submit certain information about your business (and maybe yourself). Do not start the process with the SBA loan application. Talk first with an SBA representative, or perhaps your accountant or banker, to make sure that your business is eligible for an SBA loan. Because of public policy, SBA is not permitted to make certain types of loans. Nor can it make loans under certain conditions. For example, if you can get a loan on reasonable terms from a bank, SBA cannot lend you money. The owner-manager is also not eligible for an SBA loan if he or she can get funds by selling assets that his or her company does not need in order to grow.

Most loan applications, though complex and tedious, are self-explanatory. However, some applicants have trouble with certain sections because they do not know where to go to get the necessary information. "Collateral Offered" is an example. A company's books should show the net value of assets such as business real estate and business machinery and equipment. "Net" means what you paid for such assets, less depreciation.

If an owner-manager's records do not contain detailed information on business collateral, such as real estate and machinery and equipment, the bank sometimes can get it from your federal income tax returns. Reviewing the depreciation that you have taken for tax purposes on such collateral can help arrive at the value of those assets.

If you are a good manager, you should have your books balanced monthly. However, some businesses prepare balance sheets less regularly. In filling out your "Balance Sheets as of _____ (date) Fiscal Year Ends _____ ," remember that you must disclose the condition of your business within 60 days of the date on your loan application. Your best course is to get expert advice when working up such vital information. Your accountant or banker will be able to help you.

The bank also needs information about the kinds of insurance your company carries. The owner-manager gives these facts by listing various insurance policies.

The lender will also want to know quite a bit about the personal financial condition of the applicant. Among the types of information sought are: personal cash position; source of income, including salary and personal investments (but not including alimony, which need not be disclosed); stocks, bonds, real estate, and other property owned in the applicant's own name; personal debts including installment credit payments, life insurance premiums, major periodic debt payments or other repayments which must be made. A statement of net worth (i.e., total assets in excess of total liabilities) will be very helpful and might even be demanded. If you feel the lender is asking inappropriate or questions that are too difficult, maybe you should consider another lender or try to get a cosigner whose picture is better than yours. Be very careful about financial skeletons in the closet (e.g., a judgment for an old unpaid debt). It may be best to disclose these up front with an explanation. You can certainly expect the lender to conduct a personal financial credit check unless the loan is so well protected that the personal data is insignificant.

The Lender's Evaluation

Let's say you have done your part. You have supplied both business and personal information and filled in all those nightmarish forms. The next step in the borrowing process is the evaluation by the loan evaluator (processor, loan officer) of the loan itself. He or she will look at the borrower's debt-paying record to suppliers, banks, home mortgage holders, and other creditors; the ratio of the borrower's debt to net worth, the past operations and earnings of the business, and the value and condition of the collateral that the borrower offers for security.

The factors above may be called the more tangible factors in evaluating the loan, but they are not the only factors. Among the less tangible but very important auxiliary factors in the evaluation process are the borrower's management ability, the borrower's character, and the future prospects of the borrower's business.

And don't forget, they'll be looking at you too. Your attitude, personal appearance, knowledge of your field, and ability to articulate the needs and goals of the business will all affect the decision.

One final note. Many borrowers do not succeed on their first loan attempt. This is not a sign that you or the business is not credit-worthy. It is, rather, a sign that more work and preparation is needed and that maybe you need to look for another lending source.

EQUITY FINANCING

As noted in Chapter 4, equity financing means obtaining funds in exchange for selling or giving up an ownership interest in the business. Equity financing is not a loan; rather, it is a sale of part of your business. The purchaser of equity relies upon his or her belief that buying into the business is a good investment. People or institutions who make such investments are interested in more than getting back money (i.e., the principal they lent plus the interest on that money they earn). They are interested in *potential* income rather than an immediate return on their investment. Often, equity investors become enamored with the kind of business or the growth potential of the field. They yearn for the big win. They have heard the stories of the partners of Jobs and Wozniak and Bill Gates and Ross Perot, all of whom rode the coat-tails of successful businesses that were started with a dream (and a great idea).

Equity financing has become very popular in recent years, especially in the biomedical, computer software and hardware, and other high-technology product development fields. These companies may have a product concept for which development costs can be considerable. Because start-up companies do not have the net worth, collateral or ability to repay any type of loan, they sell a portion of their business to raise money.

Chapter VII.

Understanding Commercial Transactions

"A bird in the hand is worth two in the bush."

—Old Saying

You've set up your home office, created your business plan, decided upon a legal structure, protected your assets, and procured the capital necessary to launch your business. Congratulations! You are almost ready to begin doing business. But before you rush out to sell your product or service, you should have a basic understanding of the legal implications of different types of commercial transactions.

Practically every commercial communication that can be called "doing business" involves a contract. Contracts involve the offer, acceptance and exchange of something of value (consideration). They can be oral (parol) or in writing. General contract law governs many business transactions and follows common sense. When you offer something, if it is accepted and paid for, there is a binding agreement. Most generally, you can think of these contracts as the basis for commercial transactions.

A certain subset of commercial transactions involves special contracts. We won't put you through what Charles went through as he studied the topic of sales and negotiable instruments in law school. it would not be fair to torture you that way; however, people involved in home business should have at least a general knowledge of that area of the law and business that governs commercial transactions. We shall try to make the topic of the law of commerce more interesting to you than it was to Charles. We adapted much of this material from Charles' *Legal Guide*.

Most commercial transactions in the United States are governed by the Uniform Commercial Code (UCC). The UCC, like other so-called "Uniform Laws," was a model code developed to simplify transactions among persons and organizations involving commerce in some fashion. The UCC covers a number of topic areas. The preamble to the Uniform Act refers to "Certain Commercial Transactions in or regarding personal property and Contracts and other Documents concerning them, including Sales, Commercial Paper Bills of Lading, other Documents of Title and Secured Transactions."

In other words, the UCC applies to the kinds of transactions you can expect to participate in as you do business, including purchase and sales of individual goods (i.e., consumer transactions), bulk sales (special sales not "held in the ordinary course of business"), and negotiable instruments. While the UCC is a model code, each state adopted it in some form with some variations to meet local, commercial or public policy needs. What follows are some of the generalizations that apply to the kinds of matters you will be involved in as you do business:

NEGOTIABLE INSTRUMENTS

To allow for the free flow of commerce, be it from a home-based or other business, the law has developed the concept of "negotiability" with respect to certain documents. This means that the document has legal and monetary significance on its face. Checks and promissory notes are examples of negotiable instruments. A key element in negotiability is the acceptance of the document (which lawyers call an "instrument") by the recipient in lieu of money or as evidence of money or other things of value. There are some things about the use and legal effect of these instruments every home-based businessperson should know.

A key test of negotiability in an instrument is how easily it can be transferred to another person along with the legal implications of the transfer and possession of the document. Negotiable instruments can be transferred to anyone willing to accept them and they stand on face value. If, for example, you received a note for $5,000 from Jean (an art-loving client) in exchange for a piece of artwork you created in your home studio, then you have the legal right to transfer the note to anyone who wants it.

Let's say Jason offers you $4,000 now for the note and you need the cash. The note is not due for sixty days and you can't afford to wait. You can transfer the note to Jason for the money. Jean now owes the $5,000 to Jason and must pay Jason even if Jean decides she doesn't like the painting later.

The act of transfer is referred to in this context as "negotiation" and the receipt of the instrument is known as the "holder." If the transfer has been made in the ordinary course of business the recipient is known as a "holder in due course." This means that he or she has certain legal rights flowing from the receipt of the instrument. The UCC specifies what these rights are.

Where the instrument is payable to the bearer, delivery of the instrument completes the negotiation (i.e., legal transfer). Obviously, the bearer has all the legal rights in the document without further need for action (assuming he or she received the instrument properly). A bearer instrument is virtually the same as money. Cash money is called "bearer paper." Your possession of it gives you all apparent right to use it freely.

If the instrument is not a bearer document, but, rather, is payable to a particular party (such as a check made "payable to the order of Tommy Jones"), the instrument can be negotiated only through proper endorsement by Tommy. So, following the example above, if Jason gives you a $4,000 check payable to your order and you want to pay Jessica money you owe her, you can endorse the check to her by writing in the endorsement portion: "Pay to the Order of Jessica . . ." and signing (endorsing) the check with your own name. This kind of endorsement is known as a "special endorsement" because it specifies the person to whom the instrument has been endorsed. If you merely signed your name, the endorsement is considered an "endorsement in blank."

There are other types of endorsements such as a "restrictive endorsement." Words like "For Deposit Only" or "Pay the XYZ Bank" restrict the use of the instrument and are much safer when dealing with checks. Because this is not a legal or commercial transaction treatise, we will leave you to get details on these other endorsements elsewhere.[1] The lesson here is that checks that are being accumulated for some time before deposit or are being transported should bear a special or restrictive endorsement.

Article III of the UCC specifies the formalities required to make instruments negotiable under the Code. As noted earlier, even though there may be some local laws modifying the UCC, all states have adopted the negotiability standard; therefore, in order for an instrument to be negotiable in the United States it must meet certain minimum criteria.

The instrument must be in writing and signed by the person on whose account the instrument is dependent (the "maker") or upon whom it shall be paid (the "drawer").

There must be a clear and unconditional promise to pay a sum certain in money.

The amount must be payable at a specified time clear in the instrument or "on demand" (i.e., at any time at the wish of the holder).

The instrument must be made payable to a specific person or to bearer.

Remember each of these requirements is a mandatory minimum and cannot be waived. This means that if any of these requirements is missing, the bank or maker can refuse to pay or "honor" it. Be certain before you accept a note from someone or other promise to pay, including a check, that you make sure each of the components above is clear on the face of the document.

As to checks, we felt the following checklist should help you avoid the disappointment, delay and money loss from accepting a check that proves to be no good.

---

[1] For more information on endorsements for negotiable instruments see Lickson, Charles P. *A Legal Guide for Small Business*. Menlo Park, California: Crisp Publications. 1994.

Checklist for Checks

☐ Is the check printed with the name and address of the drawer?

☐ Does the person issuing the check seem of sound mind (i.e., not under duress or under the influence of drugs or alcohol)?

☐ Is the check drawn specifically to you or is it drawn to the order of someone else and endorsed over to you? Accepting the latter carries a higher risk.

☐ Does the check bear a printed number that indicates it is not a new account? Checks with one or two digit numbers or even in the one hundred series should probably be avoided.

☐ Has the person issuing the check asked you to hold it or has he or she postdated it? If so, the chances of it not being "good" are far greater than a check issued for immediate deposit against good funds (i.e., money currently in the drawer's account).

☐ Have you ever had bad check or other bad credit experience with this person before? If so, you are forewarned and proceed at your own peril this time.

☐ Have you checked the appropriate identification of the drawer (unless that person is known to you)? Proper identification should include some type of official government picture identification if possible. Be alert to stolen ID's and aware that it doesn't take a rocket scientist to make a fake ID.

☐ Have you noted on the face of the check back-up information, such as employer name and phone, in case you need to collect on it? Some people also even make a note of the sex, birthdate, height, weight, hair and eye color and race of the person tendering the check in case they have to make an identification later to establish that the person in question issued the check. (Noting these factors for identification only does not violate any civil rights or related laws.)

State laws vary with regard to criminal sanctions for issuing "bad checks." Some jurisdictions consider most check cases civil wrongs and the state prosecutor won't help much. In other states, issuing a bad check can be a serious crime and threat of court action can yield dramatic collection results. An important caveat is in order here: before accusing a person of a crime (such as issuing a bad check) make sure you understand the local treatment of such issues. Follow recommended procedures to try to collect, such as, for example, a notice by certified mail, then request a warrant. If you are alleging a crime, you better be correct and make sure the check incident was not a genuine mistake or misunderstanding. You would not want to face a charge of malicious prosecution or defamation yourself for making an unfounded allegation.

If you expect to receive payment for goods or services by check, establish a policy about acceptance of checks by your home business. Make sure everyone who deals with collecting funds for you understands this policy. Also, learn your state's laws about bad checks and the procedure for attempting collection before you can request civil or criminal court assistance.

Keep records of the people (or firms) who have issued you bad checks. This can help prevent your next mistake and can be shared with others (as long as you are correct in your knowledge and the accuracy of the information). Remember, you don't want to libel someone by calling them a crook.

SALES

You now know that the UCC governs most commercial transactions in virtually all of the United States. When you are engaged in the sale or purchase of goods (a contract), you can expect the UCC to probably apply in some fashion. Article II of the UCC is based upon the prior law which was known as the Uniform Sales Act. Article II is structured in terms of a sales contract and the terms needed for performance.

Under the old law, delivery of property or title was the determining factor as to legal rights. Under the UCC's Article II, the written document (contract) itself controls. In fact, contracts for the sale of goods (usually in amounts of $500 or over) or those contracts that cannot be fully performed within one year are required to be in writing. This rule arose from an old English law called the "Statute of Frauds," which was designed to protect people from nefarious business practices.

Today, the Statute of Frauds is part of the UCC. Written contracts cannot be varied by evidence of prior or contemporaneous conversation or negotiations (the presumption being that the document fully reflects the agreement of the parties). See Section 2-201 of the UCC. Any modification of the deal must be in writing according to the terms of the agreement.

When a contract between parties refers to sales of goods, reference must also be made to the UCC with regard to what constitutes offer (Sec 2-205) or acceptance (Sec 2-206). Section 2-207 covers the rules regarding modifications of these types of contracts.

A warranty may be considered a separate contract within the main contract. Under warranty law, promises about the way products are or how they work are either express (actually stated) or implied by the law. Often warranties are given with regard to sales. In fact, under federal law (the Magnuson-Moss Act), specific warranty language is required for all sales of goods to consumers. This act did not replace either UCC requirements for warranties or state laws regarding consumer protection.

If you are engaged in selling products to consumers from your home business, you must become familiar with Magnuson-Moss requirements.[2]

Written warranties covering sales of products costing $15 or more must specify who the warranty covers, what part (or parts) of the product is protected, what will the warrantor pay for and what must the consumer pay for, the date of effectiveness of the warranty, if different from the purchase date, and how the consumer can obtain benefits under the warranty including addresses and instructions as to what to send, when and where.

Other provisions of the UCC covering sales include the section covering need for adequate description of goods (Sections 2-315 and 2-317), price provisions (Section 2-305), delivery time and place (Section 2-208), passage of title (Section 2-401), who shall bear the risk of loss (Sections 2-509 and 2-510) plus several other sections covering specific conditions of delivery and shipment method.

In the event of a breach of the contract of sale, both seller and buyer have remedies. These include seller's rights to react to the buyer's insolvency, repudiation of the contract, failure to cooperate and other conduct inconsistent with the sale. (If you need details, see UCC Sections 2-701 through 2-710). If the seller breaches the agreement, buyer's remedies including rights to reject goods or cancel performance are also covered in the UCC (see Sections 2-607 to 2-610 and 2-710 to 2-715).

The usual contract damages rules determine entitlement to damages for such failures of sales agreements—i.e. placing the party where he or she would have been had the agreement been lived up to. The UCC specifies other remedies in Section 2-708.

We have discussed general sales so far, but suppose the sale is pursuant to a secured transaction (i.e., title reserved in some way pending payment) or is a bulk sale (i.e., an entire inventory)? Let's take a quick look next at the legal considerations of these two important commercial transaction possibilities.

SECURED TRANSACTIONS AND CREDIT

Secured transactions are those commercial transactions where one party retains some property right in a thing of value to secure the full performance of the other's obligation. The usual kinds of secured transactions are conditional sales and loans secured by a lien on property. Using this type of financial arrangement allows some safety in extending credit from the creditor (i.e., lender) to the debtor (i.e., borrower).

---

[2] For further reading on Magnuson-Moss requirements try Lickson, Charles P. *A Legal Guide for Small Business*. Menlo Park, California: Crisp Publications, 1994.

A properly done credit arrangement secures the creditor's interest in the property pledged by the debtor even if the debtor should try to sell or transfer the property to someone else. In fact, the very rationale behind these laws is the protection of creditors from intentional or accidental loss of the security for the debt.

In looking at secured financial transactions, let's first simplify some of the language. By "secured," we simply mean that one person or firm maintains a property right in some property or thing of value of another person or firm. The term "mortgage" connotes a secured transaction, as does the term "lien." These are basically the same thing. Another term for mortgage is "deed of trust." As with all secured transactions, liens must follow certain procedure to be binding on the party to be charged (i.e., the debtor) and to serve as "notice" to the rest of the world. In this context, the term "notice" means that the law presumes that all other people dealing with the property in question know about the security interest.

Usually the permission of the debtor is required before a security interest can be "perfected" (put into place as required by law). Certain transactions can provide automatically for the institution of a lien. These kinds of transactions arise out of the working relationship between the parties. For example, if a mechanic works on your car or a carpenter works on your house, he or she may have a lien against the property for unpaid bills. Please note that while these liens arise automatically without the need for permission of the debtor, they still require certain filing to serve as notice to all others. If you are involved in a business where you may be able to get a lien by operation of law, be certain to check your local laws.

How are these security interests perfected? The UCC (Article 9) requires two basic steps to gain the legal priority of claims against the secured property. The creditor must take physical possession of the property in question and then file a financing statement in the appropriate form at the appropriate place. Check your local state laws to see where and how to file financing statements. In some jurisdictions, this is accomplished at the local or county level (usually the courthouse). In other places, the state maintains a central filing location (such as the office of the Secretary of State).

The following checklist should help you comply with the UCC conditions for secured transactions.

Secured Transaction Checklist

☐ Is the agreement in writing? (Most secured transactions must be in writing.)

☐ Does the agreement clearly identify the collateral?

☐ Are there any other claims or property interests in the collateral other than those of the debtor?

☐ Whose possession is the collateral in?

☐ Are there liens or other obligations on the debtor?

☐ What about claims of a spouse or other on the property?

☐ Will there be additions to the collateral at a future time?

☐ Which of the following Article 9 descriptions apply to the collateral?
- Goods
- Documents of title
- Accounts or other intangibles
- Items likely to become fixtures (i.e., attached to real estate, such as a bookcase affixed permanently to the wall)
- Purchase money security interest (i.e., secured debt due debtor)

☐ Does the security agreement contain sufficient language as required by the UCC?

☐ Is there a valid and properly worded loan note underlying the security claim?

☐ Has the loan note complied with all provisions of law (e.g., legal interest rate, Truth in Lending law)?

Promptness in filing the claim of security interest usually counts more than possession or even earlier legal claim to the goods. Thus, it can be a race to the Secretary of State or courthouse to file notice of secured interest.

Securing a debt under the UCC is a reasonably reliable way of making sure you will be paid. Be certain to watch for the procedural guidelines for obtaining your priority of claim against the secured goods. The office of the agency that records the claims will instruct you about the guidelines and requirements you must follow (as, of course, will an attorney versed in commercial law and many accountants).

LIENS

Some home business people may be entitled to place a lien on goods or even property. We've already discussed the lien obtained by securing collateral under the UCC. There are other liens which can be attached to property. State law governs liens. These laws are not nearly as uniform as the UCC. Lines may also arise out of common law, i.e. decisions by courts acknowledging the legality of such liens. Among these are liens for services (usually called "mechanics liens") and liens for supplies or materials (usually called "materialman's liens").

Under most states' laws, liens that arise by statute or common law (including recognized business practice) may have priority over all other liens—even those where an attempt is made to secure the loan. See UCC Section 9-310 for important information about the priority of liens.

Often the key question to arise when it comes to credit and commercial transactions is the right of a person who has no notice of someone else's alleged claim in goods. The UCC deals specifically with these issues under the notice of the "bona fide purchaser for value without notice." Laws vary as to who gets what, but it is probably fair to say that the one who has perfected a legal claim under the UCC has priority over a person who may have obtained goods in good conscience but had no perfected legal claim. This may sough tough, but the law, in its omniscience, has determined that this is the only way people can take legal comfort in commercial transactions. After all, if there is a commercial code and you have complied with it, shouldn't you be able to assert your legal rights against anyone else?

Perhaps by now you see why the topic of negotiable instruments and commercial transactions was such a nightmare to Charles in law school. If you are involved in the kind of commercial transactions that fall under the Uniform Commercial Code (as most business people are), you should get a working familiarity with the UCC provisions in your state.

We hope this chapter has unraveled a little of the mystery around these kinds of complex commercial law issues. Some homework on your own might also help in expanding your knowledge base.

ON YOUR OWN

- Think about the kind of commercial transactions your business or practice is involved in. Ask yourself whether the UCC applies to these and in what way(s).

- Discover for yourself the location in your state's statutes of the UCC and read it. If your library has the state statutes, you'll probably be able to find the UCC under the common names section finder or in the index to the statutes. Some code sections are even worth photocopying for future reference.

- If you deal in these type of transactions, contact the UCC recording agency in your state and obtain copies of the official state UCC forms (especially those that create the kinds of secured interest you might need to protect yourself someday. This is often referred to as a "UCC Form-1").

CHAPTER VIII.

What's Next? Selling or Transferring Your Business

"It's never too early to plan for the future."

—Marshall Northington

This book is by no means a guide to estate planning; however, as noted in Chapter 3, planning should include your own long-term goals. These may include your own desire to keep the business in the family and pass it along by will (estate planning), or a time may come when you want to retire or do something else. At that point you may decide to sell the business.[1]

As a rule of thumb, you should know that the longer a business had been going, the more important and significant succession planning is to the firm's continued success. Assuming that a primary goal of the home business owner is to keep the business alive and well, the importance of putting the right successor at the helm becomes paramount. This may require outside assistance from a consultant who specializes in such matters.

Needless to say, appropriate legal preparation by *inter vivos* (living) trust, gift or contract, or the proper estate plan for passing the interests of the business by will, requires the input of a first-rate probate or estate planning lawyer. There may be serious financial and tax implications which call for recommendations from an accountant or tax adviser. Choose your adviser carefully. Saving a few bucks on professional advisory fees or consultations could prove disastrous for your heirs or beneficiaries and very destructive to the business itself.

What if you decide that the business will be sold? Gill divides the business sale process into three essential steps.

---

[1] If keeping the business in the family or transferring it to a certain person or organization is your goal, you may get some excellent ideas from the chapter on succession planning from Dr. Marshall Northington's book, *Managing The Family Business* (Crisp Publications). He talks eloquently about the need for careful succession planning and offers helpful suggestions and forms.

1. Prepare yourself

2. Value your business

3. Prepare your business to be sold

Preparing yourself is easy for some people but difficult for others. Usually those who do not prepare well in advance end up losing all or most of what they could have received if they had planned to someday step aside. Your long-range business plans should include ways to prepare yourself eventually to sell your business. This planning should start at least five years in advance of the date you plan to sell your business. (Turnover within the family is a book in itself.)

One of the hardest things you may face is knowing that someday you will have to let go of "your business." Preparing ahead of time may help you overcome any reluctance about selling your business, as the planning becomes an ordinary part of doing business. However, giving up control over a business that you began and developed is difficult. One of the worst events is not getting out of your business all that you put into it. This will happen if you wait until you or someone in your family is forced to sell the business under pressure. You can avoid this if you make your retirement or exit from the business a part of your overall plan. Gill has some very good suggestions on how to do this.

1. Get yourself in the right frame of mind by planning to sell your business as a normal course of events.

2. If you decide to taper off by becoming a part of the selling package, of course do so, but remember you will not be calling the shots for everything. Plan to work only part-time on certain aspects and gradually decrease your time on the job. This should be part of the contract that also includes how much you are to be paid for your work.

3. If you do not have a hobby or other interests, develop one or more—you must have something to do besides worry about the business. There are lots of charities begging for volunteers.

4. Prepare your family. Be sure to include them in your plan so that they know you will be underfoot after a certain date. They should be included in your retirement plans.

5. Get your personal finances in order. Be sure of what you will have coming in from what ever sources will cover what you plan on doing. Check outstanding loans, continuing payments, and note any possible large purchases you may have to make. Also be sure your health and other insurance are in force and will continue as you want them to.

6. Finally make plans for right afterwards. If you are not going to continue working for a while, plan to get involved in something right away. This may be a lengthy trip, helping with your church or favorite charity or a civic association. Do something that signals that you have entered into a new part of your life—and have fun!

We have seen people feel at a loss and even become depressed after their business (their "baby") is no longer theirs. Being forewarned allows you to become forearmed.

WHAT IS THE VALUE OF YOUR BUSINESS?

Once you have decided that you are ready to sell, the next step is to determine the economic value of your business. Most of the ways to put value on a business involve very complex formulas and the use of a professional to develop them, but you can estimate a reasonable amount yourself by using a general-purpose formula. A generally accepted method is to look at four to six times the cash flow. (Cash flow is earnings before interest and taxes plus depreciation.) But this may not apply in all cases because this does not take into consideration research and development and other preoperating expenses, which may be one-time charges.

The longer you have been in business, the larger, more involved and complex your business is, the more time and help you will need to determine a fair, realistic asking price. However, the only real value of a business is the return it will bring on the new owner's investment. To calculate this, Gill suggests you use historical sales growth and earnings to project a future rate of return.

One popular formula is:

$$\frac{\text{Income} \times (1 + \text{growth})}{\text{yearly rate of return} - \text{growth}}$$

By this formula, we mean: income equals projected income, growth is the long-term rate of sales growth and the rate of return is what the buyer wants and is based on how risky the buyer perceives the investment to be.

Gill also has an excellent formula to determine income: Look at the last five or ten years' income, subtract income from other investments, expenses that are one-time-only payments, (such as insurance, a sale of part of the business or assets, any unforeseen circumstance that required unusual expenses), or anything else that would distort a true profit picture, other things being equal. If you haven't been taking a fair salary for running your business, it is appropriate to take it now. If you have paid higher wages than normal to family members for personal or family needs reasons, correct it now to bring the salary into alignment with industry standards. Do this for any extra-high rents paid or collected and any high business returns owing to weather or other such uncontrollable happenstance. Next, Gill suggests averaging these incomes and reducing the average by the expected future tax rate. This equals income under the "Gill Formula."

Gill even has good suggestions for determining your sales growth. He suggests measuring your past growth and determining an average. Chances are that if you have been in business long enough, the business should have averages of 4% to 8% in annual growth. If so, use that rate. If you can't determine your growth rate, Gill suggests that 4% is a fair rate to use (as a minimum). Obviously, if the business is in a hot, new field, projected rates of growth may be much higher. Remember Michelle Killette of GLITZ, Et Al who experienced 75% annual growth. If you actually have achieved more than 8%, know why and be able to prove it. If you can, use your figure. If you know your rate of growth was higher than 4% but cannot justify rates in excess of 8%, use the 8% rate.

Rate of return is the hardest figure to reach. If the business is risky, in fairness, this rate should be high. Here, Gill suggests the rate of return should be equal to or better than what so-called "safe" investments will bring, plus the risk factor. This is often 14% to 32%. You must select a percent that you think a future buyer will insist on. This rate of return is, in essence, a discount due the buyer because of risk. If the business can justify it, the discount will be low. If not, expect some hard bargaining for discounting from where you might expect the selling price to be.

We hope the formula information supplied above (thanks to the good work of fellow Crisp author James O. Gill) will help determine a price for the business; however, there are far more human and psychological factors to consider when the time comes for the business to pass along to someone else. Sometimes the best answer is to bring in an outside, neutral consultant to help to evaluate the value of the business and set up parameters for sale or transfer.

We hope that when you leave your business, you will be able to reap the rewards of your happy life at the home business place and have many years to watch the continuation of what you started.

CHAPTER IX.
Taxing the Home Business

"Keep it simple, Stupid."
> —Attributed to the first IRS Code Draftsman

You probably decided to operate your home business, at least in part, for purposes of simplifying your life. Well, we have sad news for you. When it comes to taxation, operating a home business can add interesting (and quite confusing) nuances to an already less than clear tax code. In the last several years, our wonderful legislators in Washington have undertaken a number of tax simplification tasks.

We don't know about you, but when we hear "simplification" coming out of Washington, we both get nervous. In fact, some would say that the term "simplified tax code" is, in itself, an oxymoron. The sad truth is that in 1913 when the first federal tax code was enacted, it numbered 15 pages. Today's tax code exceeds that slightly—by about 1,400 pages.

So before we even get started in our discussion, we must warn you to beware of oversimplification on our part. In this chapter, we have tried to supply the essence of tax laws as they may apply to you. You must not rely on us alone. Please consult a tax professional before filing any returns and/or making decisions that have tax implications (as most of your decisions will).

We have a second and very important caveat: Check the current tax code provision (yourself or by asking someone who knows) before accepting what we say here. Tax laws change routinely, but at this writing, a major overhaul of the whole United States tax structure has been proposed. Obviously, at this writing we do not know whether the overhaul will occur and, if so, how it will affect small and home-based businesses.

In great measure, some of your most important tax considerations will factor in your decision as to legal form or structure for your home business, which we covered in Chapter 4. What we offer in this section is a quick and rather simplistic review of the tax implications and ramifications of your everyday business activities and such special events as one-time capital purchases and retirement tax benefits.

Keeping in mind that you must always check on the currency of each of these points, let's now look at some of the tax factors you should know as you financially strategize for your home business.

Perhaps a logical place to start is with the use of the home as an office for tax deductibility purposes. The IRS has developed a "use test," described below. The text, including examples, is in IRS language from Booklet No. 587. We strongly suggest you obtain a copy of this booklet from your local IRS office or tax preparer.

Whether you are an employee or self-employed, you generally cannot deduct expenses for the business use of your home. But you *can* take a limited deduction for its business use if you use part of your home exclusively and regularly:

- As the principal place of business for any trade or business in which you engage

- As a place to meet or deal with patients, clients, or customers in the normal course of your trade or business

- In connection with your trade or business, if you are using a separate structure that is not attached to your residence

EMPLOYEE USE

Even if you meet the exclusive and regular use tests, you cannot take any deduction for the business use of your home if you are an employee and either of the following situations applies to you:

- The business use of your home is not for the convenience of your employer. Whether your home's business use is for your employer's convenience depends on all the facts and circumstances. However, business use is not considered for your employer's convenience merely because it is appropriate and helpful.

- You rent all or part of your home to your employer and use the rented portion to perform services as an employee.

TRADE OR BUSINESS USE

You must use your home in connection with a trade or business to take a deduction for its business use. If you use your home for a profit-seeking activity that is not a trade or business, you cannot take a deduction for its business use.

Example: You use part of your home exclusively and regularly to read financial periodicals and reports, clip bond coupons, and do similar activities for your own investments. You do not make investments as a broker or dealer. Therefore, your activities are not a trade or business and you cannot take a deduction for the business use of your home.

EXCLUSIVE USE

"Exclusive use" means only for business. If you use part of your home as your business office and also use that part for personal purposes, you do not meet the exclusive use test.

> *Example:*   You are an attorney. You use a den in your home to write legal briefs and prepare client tax returns. You also use the den for personal purposes. Therefore, you cannot claim a business deduction for using it.

Exceptions to Exclusive Use

There are two exceptions to the exclusive use test:

- The use of part of your home for the storage of inventory
- The use of part of your home as a day-care facility

STORAGE OF INVENTORY

You can deduct expenses that relate to the use of part of your home for the storage of inventory if you meet all the following five tests:

- You must keep the inventory for use in your trade or business
- Your trade or business must be the wholesale or retail selling of products
- Your home must be the only fixed location of your trade or business
- You must use the storage space on a regular basis
- The space you use must be a separately identifiable space suitable for storage

> *Example:*   Your home is the sole fixed location of your business of selling mechanics' tools at retail. You regularly use half of your basement for inventory storage and sometimes use it for personal purposes. The expenses for the storage space are deductible even though you do not use this part of your basement exclusively for business.

REGULAR USE

"Regular use" means on a continuing basis. Occasional or incidental business use of part of your home does not meet the regular use test even if that part is used for no other purpose.

PRINCIPAL PLACE OF BUSINESS

You can have more than one business location, including your home, for a single trade or business. To deduct the expenses for the business use of your home, you must determine that it is your principal place of business for that trade or business, based on all the facts and circumstances. The two primary factors are:

- The relative importance of the activities performed at each business location
- The amount of time spent at each location

The relative importance test is considered first. A comparison of the relative importance of the activities performed at each business location depends on the characteristics of each business. If the nature of the business requires that you meet or confer with clients or patients, or requires that you deliver goods or services to a customer, the place where that contact occurs must be given great weight in determining where the most important activities are performed. Performance of necessary or essential activities in your home office (such as planning for services or the delivery of goods, or the accounting or billing for those activities or goods) is not controlling.

If the relative importance test does not clearly establish the principal place of business, such as when you deliver goods or services at both the office in your home and elsewhere, then the time test is considered. The time test compares the amount of time spent on business at your home office with the amount of time spent at other locations. In some cases, there may be no principal place of business.

> *Example:* Jane Williams is an anesthesiologist. Her only office is a room in her home, which she uses regularly and exclusively to contact patients, surgeons, and hospitals by telephone; to maintain billing records and patient logs; to prepare for treatments and presentations; to satisfy continuing medical education requirements; and to read medical journals and books.

Jane spends approximately ten to fifteen hours a week doing work in her home office. She spends thirty to thirty-five hours per week administering anesthesia and postoperative care in three hospitals, none of which provide her with an office.

The essence of Jane's business as an anesthesiologist requires her to treat patients in hospitals. The home office activities, although essential, are less important to Jane's business and take less time than the services she performs in the hospitals. Her home office is not her principal place of business. Therefore, she cannot deduct expenses for the business use of her home.

MORE THAN ONE TRADE OR BUSINESS

Whether your home office is the principal place of business must be determined separately for each trade of business activity. One home office may be the principal place of business for more than one activity; however, you will not meet the exclusive use test for any activity unless each activity conducted in that office meets all the tests for the business use of the home deduction.

> *Example:* Tracey White is employed as a teacher. Her principal place of work is the school. She also has a mail-order jewelry business. She performs all her work in the jewelry business in her home office, which she uses exclusively for the business. If she meets all the other tests, she may deduct expenses for the business use of her home for the jewelry business.

If Tracey makes any use of the office for work related to her teaching, the exclusive use test is not met for the jewelry business. She may not take any home office deduction for either activity because her job as a teacher does not meet the tests for the deduction.

PLACE TO MEET PATIENTS, CLIENTS OR CUSTOMERS

If you meet or deal with patients, clients, or customers in your home in the normal course of your business, even though you also carry on business at another location, you can deduct your expenses for the part of your home used exclusively and regularly for business. You must physically meet with patients, clients, or customers on your premises and their use of your home must be substantial and integral to the conduct of your business. Occasional meetings and telephone calls do not qualify you to deduct expenses for the business use of your home.

Doctors, dentists, attorneys, and other professionals who maintain offices in their homes will generally meet the requirement.

The part of your home you use exclusively and regularly to meet patients, clients, or customers does not have to be your principal place of business.

> *Example:* Jane Quill, an attorney, works three days a week in her city office. She works two days a week in her home office used only for business. She regularly meets clients there. Her home office qualifies for a business deduction because she meets clients there in the normal course of her business.

SEPARATE STRUCTURES

You can deduct expenses for a separate free-standing structure, such as a studio, garage or barn, if you use the structure exclusively and regularly for your business. The structure does not have to be your principal place of business or a place where you meet patients, clients, or customers.

> *Example:* John Berry operates a floral shop in town. He grows the plants for his shop in a greenhouse behind his home. Since he uses the greenhouse exclusively and regularly in his business, he can deduct the expenses for its use subject to the deduction limit.

Let's look next at some general tax considerations which would apply to all small business.[1]

ACCOUNTING PERIOD: CALENDAR YEAR VS. FISCAL YEAR

We have seen from earlier discussion that every business must keep books and obviously, file tax returns based on what the IRS calls a "taxable year." The taxable year can be either a "calendar year" or a "fiscal year." A calendar year begins on January 1 and ends on December 31. A fiscal year is a twelve-month period ending on the last day of any month you choose other than December.

In fact, most small businesses use a calendar year simply because it's easier to keep track of things that way. All of the tax-relevant federal and state procedures are geared to the calendar year, such as issuance of W-2's, 1099's and dividend and interest statements, and publication of the new tax forms and instructions.

The Internal Revenue Service also prefers the calendar year. They refer to the "tax year" by the usual year date—i.e., "tax year 1996." The Internal Revenue has adopted rather complex rules about who can designate a fiscal year and when the decision must be made. The rules vary depending on how your business is legally structured. As noted earlier, generally sole proprietorships must use the same taxable year as the owner, which means the calendar year in most cases. The same rule applies to partnerships, S-corporations, and "personal service corporations" (corporations that primarily sell services performed by the owner-employees), though the Internal Revenue Service will allow these businesses to adopt a fiscal year (on Form 8716) if they have a valid business reason for using a fiscal year.

Regular (or "C") corporations can choose either a calendar or a fiscal year.

Of what value is a fiscal year? There are certain real business considerations and at least one practical reason to choose a tax year other than a calendar year. Kamaroff notes that large department stores have traditionally chosen a January 31 fiscal year so they can have their January "white sales," to reduce their stock

---

[1] Many of these points are contained in Bernard Kamaroff's excellent guide *Smalltime Operator.* Laytonville, CA. Bell Springs Publishing, 1994 (See bibliography).

of merchandise on hand, thereby making the year-end inventory count much easier and less expensive. Corporations sometimes choose a fiscal year coinciding with the month the business first began operation, in order to avoid a short-period tax return and extra taxes the fist year.

Other people choose it because their tax professionals have convinced them that it is easier for them to devote the time and attention needed for the business return without the pressure of an April 15 deadline.

For the balance of the discussion in this tax section, you can assume that the points apply to both calendar year and fiscal year taxpayers except where otherwise noted.

WHO MUST FILE A TAX RETURN?

Everyone (business or individual) must file a federal income tax return if the net earnings from self-employment (your business net profit) is $400 or more. We already know from earlier discussion how to determine net profit. If you operate more than one business and plan to file an individual (rather than corporate return), combine the profits and losses of the different businesses to arrive at the total net profit.

WHICH TAX RETURNS TO FILE

Sole Proprietors

Most sole proprietors will have to fill out Schedule C, "Profit or Loss From Business." This schedule is part of the regular 1040 return. The profit or loss on Schedule C is combined with any other taxable income or loss on your 1040.

Don't forget that some very small service businesses may only have to fill out the much simpler Schedule C-EZ, "Net Profit From Business." The form is designated "EZ" because it is easy. This form seeks one total figure for gross income, one total figure for expenses, and your net profit and a few questions about your vehicle, and that form is done!

Be careful, however, because Schedule C-EZ can only be used by **sole proprietors** who meet all ten of the following requirements:

- Gross receipts of $25,000 or less.

- Business expenses of $2,000 or less.

- No inventory at any time during the year.

- Did not have a net loss.

- Had no employees.

- Deducted no depreciation, amortization, or first-year write-off of depreciable assets.

- Deducted no expenses for a home office.

- Used the cash method of accounting.

- Owned only one sole proprietorship.

- No prior-year passive activity losses.

Partnerships

File Form 1065, "U.S. Partnership Return of Income." No taxes are due with this return. Each partner gets a copy of Schedule K-1 (1065), "Partner's Share of Income, Credits, Deductions, Etc." Partners report their individual share of the partnership income on their 1040 return, using Schedule E, "Supplemental Income and Loss."

Corporations

Regular C-corporations report income and pay taxes using Form 1120 or 1120-A.

S-corporations file Form 1120-S, but like partnerships, pay no income taxes. Each S-corporation shareholder gets a copy of Schedule D-1 (1120-S), "Shareholder's Share of Income, Credits, Deductions, Etc." Shareholders report their individual share of the S-corporation income on their own personal 1040 return, using Schedule E, "Supplemental Income and Loss."

FILING DATES FOR TAX RETURNS

For calendar-year businesses other than corporations, the federal income tax return is due April 15 — probably the best-known date in your own year except your birthday (and your anniversary, if you're smart.) For corporations, the due date is March 15.

Automatic extensions to file returns (but not to pay the taxes) are available to all businesses and individuals.

Sole proprietors and *partners* in partnerships (not the partnership itself) can obtain an automatic four-month extension, to August 15, by filing IRS Form #4868, and paying the estimated tax due, on or before April 15. Beyond the automatic four-month extension, the IRS will sometimes allow an additional two-month extension, to October 15, but only for "very good reasons" (whatever that means in the IRS psyche). File Form #2688, but only after you first file Form #4868.

Corporations can obtain an automatic six-month extension, to September 15, by filing Form #7004 and paying the estimated tax due by the March 15 due date.

Partnerships can obtain an automatic three-month extension, to July 15, by filing Form #8736 by April 15. Since partnerships pay no income taxes, no taxes are due with the extension. Partners should also file their own personal extensions on Form #4868.

All the above extensions (except Form #2688) must be filed by the original due date of the return and must include payment for all taxes which are expected to be due. If you underpay your taxes by more than 10%, the IRS will charge a penalty.

For fiscal-year businesses other than corporations, the federal income tax return is due on the fifteenth day of the fourth month following the end of the fiscal year. Corporate returns are due on the fifteenth day of the third month. The same extensions described above are available to fiscal-year businesses.

Let's not forget that states also tax businesses located there (and, in some instances, located elsewhere but doing business in the state). Many states offer extensions of time to file state returns. Some duplicate the federal rules, but some are different. To know the rules in your state, check your state income tax instruction booklet or ask your tax preparer.

BUSINESS EXPENSES

All legitimate business expenses, except those specifically disallowed by law, are deductible in computing taxable income as long as they meet the IRS's three basic rules, described well by Kamaroff:

One: These expenses must be incurred in connection with your business. Personal nonbusiness expenses are not deductible.

Two: The expenses must be, in the words of the IRS, "ordinary and necessary." Ordinary does not mean that the expense must be recurring or habitual; only that similar expenses are common or accepted in your particular type of business. A "necessary" expense, according to the IRS, is one "that is appropriate and helpful in developing and maintaining your trade or business."

Three: The amounts must be "reasonable." Expenditures that are partly personal (nonbusiness) and partly business can be prorated and the business portion expense or depreciated. Sometimes your home or your automobile fall into this category. Business expenses that you pay on your personal credit card are also fully deductible.

START-UP EXPENSES

Business expenses incurred before you start your business come under two different tax rules. They may be deductible in whole or in part, following rules of depreciation. If these expenses are considerable in your case, it will be worth the consultation with a tax professional. If they are relatively minor, such as purchase of books and reports about the potential business, they are probably not deductible and may not be worth the aggravation and expense to create deductibility.

As Kamaroff notes, "the IRS has often wrangled with taxpayers over which costs are and aren't 'start-up—and at what point a new venture is actually 'in business.' The IRS has stated that a business hasn't actually started until it produces income. Tax courts have disagreed and have ruled that once a business is set up and 'open for business,' it is officially started even if it has not made a sale yet." Kamaroff, a C.P.A., suggests that you discuss this with an accountant.

With regard to deductibility of business expenses, check with your tax preparer or look at Section Four in Kamaroff's book. We will not detail them here because there is much change afoot regarding deductibility. Suffice it to say that if the expenses are legitimately related to the production of income, they are probably deductible. There are some limitations (e.g., 50% of business entertainment) and exceptions.

One important note about deducting home office expenses: If your home business shows a loss, part of your home office expenses are not deductible this tax year. The rule is that a home business may deduct any regular business expenses (other than expenses attributable to the office itself) and may deduct interest and property taxes on the home office, regardless of profit or loss. But the remaining home office expenses (rent or depreciation, insurance, utilities) may be deducted the year they are incurred only to the extent there is no loss.

Be careful! Not every expense is deductible.

NONDEDUCTIBLE EXPENSES

Certain expenses are specifically disallowed by law and cannot be deducted on your income tax return. Many of these are obvious, but are listed here anyway.

- Expenses not related to your business, and business expenses not meeting the "ordinary and necessary" or the "reasonable" test.

- Federal income tax and any tax penalties; however, interest on back taxes may or may not be deductible. State income tax is deductible on your federal return but not on your state return.

- Any fines or violation of the law. For example, a parking fine cannot be deducted even if you incurred the charge while on business.

- Clothing, unless used exclusively for work and unsuitable for street wear such as a uniform or blazer with business logo.

- Regular meals at work (although there are some exceptions).

- Usual and customary commuting expenses between your home and usual place of business.

- Cost of land (until you sell it); however, the structure on the land may be depreciated.

If you think the foregoing is confusing, wait, there's more . . .

SELF-EMPLOYMENT TAX (SEA)

Self-employment tax, also known as SEA (Self Employment Contributions Act), is, in actuality, Social Security/Medicare tax for self-employed individuals. Unfortunately, independent business people pay the highest Social Security/Medicare rates of all, and they go up every year. Self-employment tax is based on your net profit, the taxable net income of your business.

Sole proprietors (including independent outside contractors and freelancers) and partners in partnerships are subject to self-employment tax. The tax is not imposed on corporations; so, if you own a small corporation, and you are an employee of your business, it will pay regular Social Security and Medicare instead of self-employment tax (any director's fees not included as part of a regular salary are subject to the self-employment tax). Rental income, interest, and other nonbusiness income are not subject to self-employment tax.

Self-employment tax is not federal income tax. It stands on its own. You may owe no income tax but still be liable for self-employment tax. Retirement deductions, deductions for health insurance, and the regular personal deductions and exemptions, which reduce income tax, cannot be used to reduce self-employment tax. Be careful of this one. It takes people by surprise very often. As Kamaroff alerts us, "People, particularly in part-time and sideline businesses, are not making enough profit to worry about income taxes, but they never realize they may have a substantial self-employment tax bill."

A note for the very small business: if your business profits are $400 or less, you do not have to pay any self-employment tax. But, if you net $401, you pay self-employment tax on the entire $401, not just the one dollar over the $400 minimum. If you made $400 or less but want to pay self-employment tax, to increase your Social Security account, the IRS provides an optional method where by you can pay into Social Security and Medicare. It is explained on the SE tax form, which you obtain like any other IRS form or pamphlet.

RETIREMENT FUND TAX CONSIDERATIONS

In all likelihood, you will want to invest a portion of your business profit in a special retirement plan and, if possible, not be liable to pay income taxes on the money invested or the interest until you retire and withdraw the funds. Presumable, your financial tax bracket will be lower at that time.

Kamaroff describes the three principal tax-deferred retirement plans available to business owners: "The Self Employed Retirement Plan," commonly called

Keogh or H.R. 10 plan (named for the congressman who sponsored it and his bill number); the SEP, "Simplified Employee Pension Plan"; and the IRA, "Individual Retirement Account." You should consider, in deciding which plan is best for you, the different options, different maximum contributions, different deadlines for making contributions and, most important to employers, different requirements for including your employees in the plan. The rules permit you to set up a Keogh or an SEP, but not both; however, depending on your income, you may be able to set up an IRA in addition to a Keogh or SEP.

Let's look next at these options in more detail

IRA

The best-known and simplest plan to initiate is the Individual Retirement Account. Any taxpayer, whether business owner or wage earner, can set up an IRA. The maximum annual contribution is only $2,000 or your taxable earnings, whichever is less. If you or your spouse have an outside job that includes a retirement plan, be aware that the allowable IRA deduction may be even less than $2,000. As a business owner, an IRA does not create any obligation to cover any of your employees. You can set up or contribute to an IRA any time up to the date your tax return is due (April 15 of the next year).

SEP

While the IRA is easiest to establish, a Simplified Employee Pension Plan is also easy to set up. Under an SEP, you can invest up to 13.04% of your earnings every year, up to a maximum investment of $22,500 a year. At this writing, the tax law actually says that the maximum is 15%, but, as Kamaroff points out, "the convoluted way of computing the contribution works out to 13.04%. You can set up or contribute to an SEP right up to the due date of your tax return (April 15 of the next year, or later if you file an extension), applying the deduction to the previous year's income."

An important distinction between IRA and SEP should be noted. Under an SEP, the employer must include all employees over twenty-one years old who have worked for the firm three of the last five years. The SEP must also include part-time and occasional employees.

Who actually pays for the employee's SEP plan depends on how the plan is set up. Under the regular SEP plan, the employer pays the full cost of the plan. The employer contributes the same amount or percentage for each eligible employee as he or she does for him or herself. An SEP has other nuances that may alter this payment ratio. Ask your tax professional about the SEP Salary Reduction Arrangement. These arrangements may cost the employer nothing other than the extra paperwork. Only smaller businesses (25 or fewer employees) are eligible for the Salary Reduction Arrangement. One bit of good news: any money an employer invests in an SEP on behalf of employees is a tax-deductible business expense.

Keogh

There are several versions of Keogh plans and they are far more complicated than the two above, with more paperwork and more government forms to file. You will probably need help in setting them up and understanding them. There are a number of sources available to help you (including a very good chapter in Kamaroff's book). The Keogh plans offer larger contributions and different requirements for including employees. For some businesses, a Keogh plan will be more than worth the extra trouble.

We cannot provide details of Keogh plans here due to the complexity of the qualification and set-up. We wanted you to know about them and to be able to ask an adviser about them if you feel they may be more suitable than either of the other plans.

In sum, IRAs are for individuals, sole proprietors and partners in partnerships. SEPs and Keoghs are available to all businesses, including corporations, but the maximum deductions, limitations, etc., for corporations may differ from those described above. There are also special corporate retirement plans you can set up, quite different from those described here. Again, a financial planner or employee benefits professional can be of great assistance here.

If as principal of your home business you are an employer, please note the following:

If you want to set up a retirement plan just for yourself, without having to pay your employees' retirement, there is good news and bad. The good news is that many insurance companies offer "nonqualifying plans" of all types. The bad news is that under those "nonqualifying plans" (so called because they do not qualify for an income tax deduction) you must pay regular income taxes on your entire business profit. You are not allowed any tax deduction.

HOW TO DEVELOP A RETIREMENT PLAN

Most banks and insurance companies offer IRA, SEP and Keogh plans. Each plan will be different, and the earned interest can vary with different plans and amounts. As noted above, seek professional guidance from an independent source (as opposed to those who would sell you their plan). For general information, the IRS publishes two free booklets, Pub. 590, *Individual Retirement Accounts* (which also covers SEPs); and Pub. 560, *Self-Employed Retirement Plans* (Keoghs).

There may be other credits available to you from your home business. Be certain to talk to your tax preparer if you have suffered a loss (either from regular business operations or a special casualty such as fire or flood). Be sure also to ask about tax credits and other potential deductions, including depreciation for capital expenditures.

In closing this section, we wanted to remind you that unfortunately, the tax bite doesn't just come from Uncle Sam. Uncle State takes some and even Uncle

City or County (in some areas). Watch out for state income taxes, licenses fees, business licenses and related fees and charges. These will be needed and charged often without regard to profit (or loss) from your business.

You must make an effort to find out about your state's tax laws on small businesses. In addition to asking a tax professional, there are several other ways of getting the information, such as calling state offices, asking other business owners, or visiting the library.

There are those who never mind paying taxes because it shows they're earning their keep in their country and local area. There are others who hate to pay taxes no matter what. Wherever you are on the spectrum, be certain to prepare for the tax bite. Getting short on cash at tax time can literally destroy a home business and not paying required taxes (such as withholding taxes for employees) can send you on an unwanted vacation at government expense.

A Final Note

"Light is the task where many share the toil."

—Homer

We know you have done a great job reading and digesting some of the suggestions in this book. We're sure that over the course of this book you have wondered about special financial situations facing your specifically in your work. We designed this book to generate not only answers but also questions. We hope you have found many answers in these pages but we know that a number of strategic financial issues simply cannot or, for that matter, should not, be handled by you alone. So what do you do?

You find out how and where you can get answers and/or assistance from the outside. Go for help with the same determination you had when you first tried to figure out how to handle the situation yourself.

The appendices that follow are by no means exhaustive, but they should give you a good start in your quest for aid in resolution of your unanswered business-related questions.

In most areas, the first place to look for assistance with a business management or financial question is your accountant or other financial resource person.

Good luck!

We are so pleased that as teachers and trainers we can brag about good and continuing relationships with our students and trainees. One of the things we find most useful in creating such a good feeling is the fact that once a course or training program is over for us, it does not mean that it is the end of communication between us and the student/participant.

We want that process to continue with you too. You have now read this book. We hope you found it valuable. If you have questions, comments or need some information you think we can provide, feel free to contact us directly at (540) 636-2515.

We salute your success in your home business and your other endeavors!

Glossary

This glossary covers some of the more common terms used in business and commercial financial transactions. These are our definitions and they are intentionally not presented in technical language. [1]

ACCEPTANCE. The indication of willingness to enter into a contract.

ACCOUNTS PAYABLE. Sums owed and unpaid to suppliers of goods and services to the business.

ACCOUNTS RECEIVABLE. Sums owed to the business from the sale of goods and services that have not yet been paid.

ACCOUNTING SYSTEM. The methodology for determining which accounting basis the business uses (i.e., accrual or cash. See below.)

ACCORD. An agreement.

AGREEMENT. The outcome of a successful discussion, negotiation or other process that represents the meeting of the minds of the parties with respect to the subject matter. It may be oral or in writing and is usually binding unless expressed otherwise.

ACCRUAL BASIS ACCOUNTING. It records the sale, expense or other event when it actually occurs, rather than when the money changes hands. Under this basis, it is not the actual receipt of payment that is important but the "right" to receive it. Compare it to cash basis accounting. (See below).

---

[1] Many of the terms used in this glossary are described in Covello [pp. 137–145], Gill and the *Legal Guide.* If you need more detailed definitions, check the written resources we've cited and Money's *Complete Guide to Personal Finance and Investment Terms* compiled by John Downes and Jordan Elliot Goodman [Woodbury, NY, Barrons Educations Series, 1985.]

ADMINISTRATIVE EXPENSE. Usual operating expenses such as salaries, stationery, postage, office supplies, telephone, insurance, depreciation of office equipment, and rent.

ALTERNATIVE DISPUTE RESOLUTION (ADR). Nonlawsuit procedure for resolving disputes, such as mediation or arbitration.

AMORTIZATION. The gradual payment of a debt through a schedule of payments or the process of writing off an intangible asset against expenses over the period of its economic useful life.

AUDIT. A review of all or part of the business's financial status usually prepared by or at the request of someone outside the business.

AUDITED FINANCIAL STATEMENT. A report on the business's financial status obtained after independent review of transactions by a qualified outside accountant or auditor.

ARBITRATION. The process whereby the parties to a dispute designate a neutral third person to hear the issue and render a decision. The parties may decide in advance whether that decision will be binding. Arbitration is considered an Alternative Dispute Resolution procedure.

ASSIGN. To transfer some interest in something.

BAILMENT. A delivery of goods under an agreement that the goods be cared for reasonably by the bailee (one who receives the goods).

BAD DEBT. Debts to the business that are either uncollectable or likely to be uncollectable.

BALANCE SHEET. The document that describes the assets, liabilities and net worth of the company at a fixed time.

BANKRUPTCY. Either a formal proceeding whereby debtor seeks discharge or release form certain debts. Can also mean failure to meet current obligations when due or liabilities exceeding assets.

BILL OF LADING. Both a receipt and a contract by a common carrier that goods have been received for shipment.

BINDING. The agreement of the parties to give full legal effect to their outcome.

BOARD OF DIRECTORS. A group of individuals, elected by stockholders, who as a body manage the corporation. Directors elect officers who manage the everyday affairs of the corporation.

BREAK-EVEN ANALYSIS. The method of financial analysis used to determine the exact point at which the business operates without either a loss or profit but merely meets all expenses when due.

BREACH. Breaking a law or regulation or any duty. Violation of a contract.

BUDGET. The plan for all or part of the business for allocation of revenues and expenses over a specific period of time.

BUSINESS PLAN. A document that describes the business, its objectives, strategies, operating plans, environment, marketing strategies, essential players and significant financial data. It is often described as "the road map" for managing the business.

BUSINESS RECEIPTS. Sales and/or receipts from the operations of the business.

CAVEAT EMPTOR. Latin term for "let the buyer beware."

CAPITAL. The general term for monies invested into a business enterprise.

CASH BASIS ACCOUNTING. Under this method, the transaction is recorded only when the cash payment is received, as compared to accrual basis accounting (see above).

CASH FLOW ANALYSIS. The systematic charting of the sources and uses of cash in a business over a designated period of time.

CERTIFIED PUBLIC ACCOUNTANT (CPA). A financial professional who has passed qualifying exams and meets required professional and state regulatory requirements.

CHECK. Written instructions or order to a bank to pay.

COLLATERAL. Personal or business assets the borrower assigns to the lender to guarantee debt payment.

CONVERTIBLE LOAN. A loan to the business whereby the lender has the option of repaying the loan or taking part ownership (equity) in the business.

CORPORATION. An organization formed under a state statute for the purpose of carrying on an enterprise in such a way as to make the enterprise distinct from the persons who control it. For legal purposes, a corporation has many of the attributes of a person.

CONSIDERATION. The thing of value exchanged that makes a contract valid.

CONTRACT. A legal binding mutual undertaking. See text.

CONVEY. To formally transfer title.

COST OF GOODS AND/OR SERVICES. Cost directly associated with making or providing the goods or services. It usually includes raw material costs, building costs, machine costs, and other variable overhead.

CURRENT ASSETS. Cash, marketable securities, accounts receivables, inventory and other assets owned by the business that can be liquidated quickly.

CURRENT LIABILITIES. Debts that must be met within a relatively short time, usually within one year, such as short-term loans, accounts payable, professional fees, wages payable, and accrued taxes.

CUSTOMER PROFILE. Description of the customer, including type, characteristics and habits.

CYCLICALITY. The variations in business revenue related to economic conditions and seasons.

DEED. A document transferring title (usually to real estate); must be executed in a formalized manner described by statute.

DEBT FINANCING. The use of borrowed money to finance a business. The loan is repaid in the form of principle and interest; the lender receives only cash back and no ownership of the business.

DEFAULT. An unwillingness or inability to live up to a legal obligation.

DEMOGRAPHICS. Profiling clients or customers by age, sex, family size, income, occupation, education, religion, culture, social class, etc.

DEPRECIATION. The process of expensing the decreased value of a fixed asset over its useful life. Its primary significance is for credit from taxes; however, it can also help determine when to replace the asset.

DIRECT LABOR. Labor costs directly associated with production or contract work in creating the product or service.

DOUBLE-ENTRY BOOKKEEPING. A bookkeeping method where transactions are first entered in a journal or log, then posted to ledger accounts to show income, expenses, assets, liabilities and net worth. Each account classification allows for the recording of debits and credits. May be used with computerized as well as manual systems.

DOWNLINE. People who make up part of the representative's own personal network marketing or MLM organization and who do business with the company through him or her. See MLM and Upline.

ENDORSE. The act by which a negotiable instrument is passed along—i.e., writing one's name on the back of a check or draft.

EQUITY. The net value of assets minus liabilities; also known as net worth. Term can also mean an ownership interest in a business; also a system which serves as an auxiliary to the law (but available in a court of law) to prevent injustice in civil matters.

EQUITY FINANCING. The securing of monies from an investor in which the investor becomes part owner of the business. The investor would expect a share in the profits of the business rather than return of monies lent with interest (see "debt financing").

EXIT PROGRAM OR STRATEGY. The preplanned program for an investor to exit a venture by turning his or her investment into cash or another easily traded instrument.

ESCROW. Turning over something of value to a third party who acts as an agent for the parties to hold the money or goods until certain conditions are met.

FIDUCIARY. A person or organization in a special trust relationship with another.

FISCAL YEAR. The year end (usually consists of a twelve-month period), established by a business for accounting, planning, and tax purposes. It does not necessarily correspond with a calendar year.

FINANCIAL REPORTS. Reports that show the financial status of a company at a given time.

FINANCIAL STATEMENT. A written presentation of financial data prepared from the accounting records. Statements include a balance sheet, income statement (or profit and loss statement), and cash flow statement. May be prepared by the business itself or an outside professional such as a CPA.

FIRST IN–FIRST OUT (FIFO). An accounting and economics term used to describe the method of valuing inventory. Assumes that the goods first acquired are the goods first sold. FIFO is the most commonly used method for inventory valuation.

FIXED ASSET. Usually large tangible items such as equipment, buildings, machinery, vehicles, and leasehold improvements that are used in the business.

FIXED COSTS. Those business costs that do not vary whether or not revenue fluctuates.

FORECASTING. The systematic calculation of all reasonable probabilities about the business future.

FRANCHISE. A business that is contractually bound to operate on another companies' image, concept and guidelines.

GENERAL ADMINISTRATIVE EXPENSES. Expenses that are directly associated with the management of the business and not with making and/or selling the product or service.

GOODWILL. An intangible asset related to the perceived value of the business assets by others.

GRANT. The passage of something from one to another.

GUARANTOR. A person who serves as surety for another.

INCOME STATEMENT. A generally accepted accounting format for determining the profit and loss of a business; usually generated yearly, quarterly, or monthly.

INDEMNITY. To secure a person or firm against loss.

INSIDE SALES FORCE. Those personnel who are in direct contact with clients or customers (often by phone or online) but who do not leave their place of work in the performance of their duties.

INTANGIBLE ASSET. Assets that do not have a physical presence but have value, such as goodwill, logos, trademarks, patents, copyrights, designs, image, formulae, franchises, brands, customer lists, and mailing lists.

INTEREST. The amount paid by the borrower as a premium for borrowed money.

INTERIM FINANCING. Acquisition by the business of funds for a short term when it is planned that by the end of that period, necessary financing of a longer term will be provided.

INVENTORY. Items that have been produced or purchased now in the possession or control of the business but that will ultimately be sold. These would include raw material inventory, work in progress inventory, and finished goods inventory.

INVENTORY FINANCING. The process of obtaining needed capital for a business by borrowing money with inventory used as collateral.

JOINT VENTURE. Collaborative undertaking or partnership between two or more businesses to accomplish some task or business.

JUDGMENT. A final binding order of court, the outcome of legal proceedings.

LAST IN–LAST OUT (LIFO). Another method for inventory valuation. Assumes that the units sold are the most recently acquired and that the units on hand are those first acquired. (Compare to First In–First Out.)

LEVERAGE. The use of credit or borrowing power of a principal or business to increase the ability to conduct business.

LIEN. A right asserted against or upon something allowing possession until the obligation underlying it is satisfied.

LINE OF CREDIT. An advance commitment by a bank or other financial resource to lend up to the amount agreed upon.

LIQUIDITY. The amount of cash that can be generated in a short time from the conversion of assets by sale, loan or exchange.

MANAGEMENT CONSULTANT. An expert or specialist outside a business who advises the business on management matters. According to Covello, professional management consultants have three basic advantages over a business's own officers and employees:

1. They bring in a point of view attained by experience with many enterprises; they can see things in proper perspective.

2. Their approach to problems is generally impartial, but it is advisable for management, when retaining a consultant, to emphasize that a predetermined result is not being sought.

3. Since such investigations are the consultant's operations, effort are more concentrated on your investigation.

MARKET. A clearly defined group of people, area, or group of things that can be classified together as having some commonality and that represents an area of potential revenue for the business.

MARKET ANALYSIS. The method of determining the characteristics of the market and the measurement of its capacity to buy products and services.

MARKETING. The act of identifying, performing, persuading, and satisfying the needs of the clients or customers.

MARKETING PLAN. The combination of a market analysis and marketing strategies that defines both clients or customers and competitors and that describes how the business will reach and close with its clients or customers.

MARKET SHARE. The revenue of your business divided by the total revenue from your field or industry for either your local market or national or international market. Market share is usually expressed as a percentage of the total industry.

MEDIATION. The process whereby a neutral third party selected by the disputants assists them in reaching accord through distinct procedural steps designed to develop agreement. The parties set the groundrules and may agree to be bound or not. It is a recognized ADR process achieving ever-increasing support.

MISREPRESENTATION. The intentional misstatement of present facts designed to induce someone to do something.

MISSION STATEMENT. The defined goal of the business or practice as outlined in a written statement of purpose.

MORTGAGE. A conveyance of legal title to property (usually land) to serve as collateral for a debt.

MULTILEVEL MARKETING (MLM). A segment of the economy that does business through a hierarchical marketing structure. Now better known as "Network Marketing." See also "Upline" and "Downline."

NEGLIGENCE. A tort action, the failure to live up to a duty, causing injury and damages. Must be proximately connected to the alleged misconduct.

NEGOTIABLE. That aspect of a financial instrument that allows it to freely pass in commerce.

NEGOTIATION. The act of passing along a negotiable instrument; also, a term used to describe active and committed discussion designed to reach specific goals.

NET PROFIT AFTER TAXES. Net profit before taxes less federal, state or local income or franchise taxes.

NET PROFIT BEFORE TAXES. Net sales or total receipts less all expenses, including interest but without allocation for taxes.

NET REVENUE OR SALES. Total sales or revenues less discounts, returned goods, and pricing allowances.

NET WORTH. The value of assets of the business less liabilities. Net worth is sometimes referred to as the "equity" in the business but this is contrasted to "equity" as defined above.

NET WORTH OF A CUSTOMER. A calculated formula used to indicate the dollar value of a client's or customer's patronage every time he or she buys from or uses the services of the business.

NETWORK MARKETING. The more current term for Multilevel Marketing. See "MLM."

NOTES PAYABLE. An account in the liability section of the general ledger showing the amount of money owed by the business as evidenced by negotiable promissory notes incurred by the business.

NOTES RECEIVABLE. An account in the asset section of the general ledger showing the amount of money owed to the business as evidenced by negotiable promissory notes received from clients or customers in payment for goods sold and delivered or others in the ordinary course of business (such as vendors or suppliers).

OPERATING EXPENSES. Those expenses of the business that are not directly associated with the making or providing of the goods or services. These usually include administrative, technical and selling expenses.

OPERATIONS. The daily, weekly or monthly activities that comprise the working functions of the business. An "Operational Plan" sets forth the plan for running the business over a pre-planned period of time.

OUTSIDE SALES FORCE. Personnel who perform the selling function and meet with clients or customers either at the clients' or customers' location or outside the usual business office.

PAROL. Oral.

PARTNERSHIP. The Uniform Partnership Act defines the arrangement as an "association of two or more persons to carry on as coworkers of a business for profit."

PATENT. An exclusive right granted by the federal government to make, use, and sell an invention for a fixed period of time. Patents are sometimes referred to as "legal monopolies." A patent can protect an idea itself whereas a copyright is usually limited to the expression of an idea.

PLEDGE. A promise signified by the giving of goods such as in bailment.

POWER OF ATTORNEY. Assignment to another of legal power to undertake specified activity on behalf of the assignor.

PREFERRED STOCK. Stock that is given a preference over other forms of stock within the same corporation, primarily with respect to dividend payments and, on occasion, upon liquidation of the company. Preferred stock may be voting or nonvoting.

PRO FORMA. A projection of future activity of the business. This term is most often associated with a business's financial projections.

PROJECTED FINANCIALS. An estimation of future financial earnings and expenses utilization pro forma data (see above).

PROPRIETORSHIP (SOLE PROPRIETORSHIP). An individual owner of a business who has not incorporated, nor has a recognized partner. Under this legal form the owner is liable for all the debts of the business to the full extent of his or her own property.

PUBLIC OFFERING. Offering of shares of stock (or limited partnership interests) of the business to the public. Public offerings are strictly regulated by the Securities and Exchange Commission at the federal or nationwide level and by state securities or banking commissions at the state level. State securities laws are referred to as Blue Sky statutes.

QUASICONTRACT. An implied contract created by the acts of the parties.

QUICK RATIO. Cash plus Accounts Receivable divided by current liabilities.

REORGANIZATION. A process involving a recasting of corporate capital structure, including debt consideration, which the corporation may be compelled to undergo because of either imminent or immediate insolvency. Under federal bankruptcy laws, reorganization is undertaken pursuant to Chapter 11. (See also "Bankruptcy" above.)

RETAINED EARNINGS. Net profit after taxes that is retained in the business as working capital and not paid out as dividends to stockholders.

RETURN ON EQUITY. Profit on the total equity in the company.

RETURN ON GROSS OPERATING ASSETS. Profit on the total assets used in the business.

RETURN ON INVESTMENT (ROI). That profit or gain obtained by the investor above and beyond his or her cash investment.

REVENUES. Used interchangeably with Sales. Often used for businesses that do not physically sell something, such as service businesses or professional practices.

ROYALTY. The agreed payment to a licenser or grantor of rights to sell, publish or otherwise use one's rights.

SECURITIES AND EXCHANGE COMMISSION (SEC). Federal government body that is chartered to maintain order and rules of the stock and securities exchanges. The SEC rules govern all interstate sales of securities (i.e., shares in a business and some franchise interests).

SEED CAPITAL. Those funds invested or loaned that allow the business to launch.

SELLING EXPENSES. Expenses incurred in selling or distributing a product or service.

SETTLEMENT. An agreement that represents the successful outcome of a discussion, negotiation or ADR process and that ends the dispute.

SMALL BUSINESS ADMINISTRATION (SBA). An independent agency of the federal government, under the general direction and supervision of the executive branch. The SBA is authorized to furnish credit either as a maker of a direct loan, or, more usually, as a guarantor in part of a loan made by a bank to a business.

SPECIFIC PERFORMANCE. The order of court to parties to perform the contract as written.

STRATEGIC OPPORTUNITY. An opportunity or goal that can change the basic thrust (long-term strategies) of the business.

STRATEGY. The basic method to reach a defined goal.

STATUTE OF LIMITATIONS. The time limits set by the legislature within which certain actions may be brought to the courts.

STOCK. Can refer to the product inventory of a business; also describes the certificate of equity ownership in a corporation.

SUIT. The action in the courts.

TELECOMMUTER. One who operates on behalf of another from home or another off-site location through use of computer communications.

TERM. The length of running of a contract.

TORT. An actionable, noncontract legal wrong.

TRADE RECEIVABLES. See Accounts Receivable.

TRADE PAYABLES. See Accounts Payable.

TRUST. The basis for special reliance; also a form by which something is held for the benefit of someone else.

TRUSTEE. A fiduciary who is asked to administer a trust for the benefit of another.

UNEMPLOYMENT INSURANCE. A federal-state system that provides temporary income for workers when they are unemployed due to circumstances beyond their control. Businesses contribute to the plan through payroll deduction from employees and supplements by the business.

UNIQUE SELLING ADVANTAGE (USA). Defined by Covello as: "The essential appeal a business owner develops to share with staff members and clients or customers. It is all the unique reasons why clients or customers should buy from your company, all stated in one crisp, easy-to-understand paragraph."

UNSECURED LOAN. A loan made with no actual collateral or security posted to guarantee payment of the loan.

UPLINE. Those people higher in a network marketing organization through whom the representative does his or her business. See MLM and Downline.

USURY. An unlawfully high rate of interest.

VARIABLE COST. Costs that vary directly with sales or revenues. Examples of variable costs are: raw material costs, certain utility costs, labor, sales commissions, and advertising.

VARIANCES. An accounting term for the difference between what was forecast and what actually happened. "Variance" in real estate law refers to a special permission to nonconform to zoning requirements.

VENTURE CAPITAL. A pool of investment monies sometimes made by institutions but most often made by private investors who provide monies needed by the business to follow its plan. Venture capitalists also often advise business on ways to enhance the business (and their investment). Venture capitalists will often require controlling or a majority voting interest in the company.

VOID. Of absolutely no legal force or effect.

VOIDABLE. May result in no legal affect if asserted.

WARRANTY. A special undertaking in an agreement.

WORKING CAPITAL. Generally accepted financial term for current assets less current liabilities.

Resources

In most areas, the first place to look for assistance with a home business problem is a professional business management consultant.

How do you find a consultant or adviser if you don't already have one?

The best way is to ask someone you trust for the name of a qualified professional experienced in the field of business or commercial law. Any successful home-based business or professional person will have had dealings with an attorney. Some of his or her experiences will have been good—others will not have been so good, but all in all, most successful people surround themselves with competent professional advisers including attorneys and accountants.

If you do not know anyone to ask, consult the chamber of commerce, business development agency or college. They may even have a referral or consulting service that should function in a professional, nonbiased manner, designed to give you the name of an adviser experienced in your area of interest.

Remember that there are state commerce and business development agencies and associations in some areas and local associations in most urban areas. There are also business and commercial groups and associations who are listed below.

If you live near a college or university, don't feel shy about contacting the business school (if it has one) or the business or commercial department of the general academic program for the name of an attorney and consultant experienced in business. Often, an adjunct member of the faculty (especially at community colleges) is a practicing attorney or successful business person and can help. Beware of the novice. It is not easy finding work as a lawyer these days and some lawyers are teaching (not because they have great legal backgrounds to share, but rather because they can't find anything else to do—or they just want to teach). These folks may be great teachers but it is not too likely that you will get sophisticated advice from the sometimes-lawyer-who-teaches (or the sometimes-teacher-who-lawyers).

Advertising is now permitted for lawyers (as well as many other professions), so you might try the Yellow Pages. Some attorneys are permitted by their local rules to list fields they practice in. Check to see whether the listing implies special knowledge or qualifications in the filed of specialty. Most bar associations require lawyers who advertise specialties to be specially qualified or to use warning words that they are only claiming an interest in a particular field. Virtually every telephone directory has a listing for consultants. Many break that category down further to business consulting and other specialties. Again, be careful. Often, the most successful consultants do not need to and are reluctant to advertise. We advise word of mouth as the best way to find assistance.

For general information on business and government programs, contact the organizations listed below.

Economic Development Administration
U.S. Department of Commerce
Washington, DC 20230
(202) 377-5081

Minority Business Development Agency
U.S. Department of Commerce
Washington, DC 20230

Small Business Administration
1441 L Street, NW
Washington, DC 20416
(202) 653-6385
(800) 433-7212

American Association of Minority Enterprise
Small Business Investment Companies
915 15th Street, NW
Washington, DC 20005
(202) 347-8600

National Small Business Association
1604 K Street, NW
Washington, DC 20006
(202) 296-7400

National Association of Small Business Investment Companies
1156 15th Street, NW
Washington, DC 20005
(202) 833-8230

SCORE

The Service Corps of Retired Executives (SCORE) has more than 12,000 volunteer members in 592 offices around the county to advise prospective business owners, regardless of age or status. Call (800) 368-5855 to find an office near you.

For financial data on firms and ratio and percentage information, contact:

Dun and Bradstreet, Inc.
Public Relations Department
99 Church Street
New York, NY 10007

For information on special needs and employment supports, especially regarding work at home, contact your state office of rehabilitation, the IBM Special Needs Information Referral Center in Atlanta at (800) 426-3333, or Apple Worldwide Disability Solutions Group at (800) 732-3131.

Bibliography

There are a number of very good and easy-to-read books about business in general, a few good ones about home business, a larger number that discuss financial issues for small business and several decent guides for business people about law. Of course, as with every technical subject there are student texts and scholarly treatises as well. We have purposely avoided citing below the texts and treatises.

If you are serious about the subject, many larger urban libraries, most university libraries and almost all decent-sized companies have their own business library. If you live near a business school, you will find yourself in law library heaven. In any of these libraries you will find relevant books and journals (and even management case studies) on virtually every topic of business, and you will also probably find a terminal for the more popular online data information systems available. Of course, accessing these systems may not be too easy. You first need permission, then a log-on identifier, and then you must know how to organize a search. The librarian or a nearby student (who probably is playing computer games and should be studying anyway) can help.

In the interest of assisting your further reading on this topic, we have listed below a number of books we found helpful both in preparing this book for you and in supporting our own successful businesses.

As mentioned in the text, much of the legal information in this work can be found in its original and more generic form in Lickson, *A Legal Guide for Small Business* (Menlo Park, CA, Crisp Publications, 1995.) Other law-related books we used were:

Anderson, *Business Law (Eleventh edition)*, (Cincinnati, South-Western Publishing Co., 1980). This text covers all the basics. Look for a later edition.

Barnes, Dworkin and Richards, *Law for Business (Third Edition)* Homewood, IL, Richard D. Irwin, Inc. 1987). This is an excellent student text and was appreciated by my students and their teacher.

Dungan and Ridings, *Business Law*, (New York, Barrons, 1990). This small and handy book is part of the Barron's Business Library and highly recommended. Watch the date. Sometimes, legal information can become stale quite quickly due to changing laws or late decisions.

As to financial and business strategy issues, we heartily recommend all the titles in the Crisp Small Business Series, especially the particular series titles we used as resources. The Crisp titles by Bivins, Martin and Northington were especially helpful. There are also several other publishers who have very handy series for small business people. These include Nolo Press, Sourcebooks, and Bell Springs Press, some of whose books are listed below. In preparing this book, we used and recommend the following:

Alarid, William M. *Money Sources for Small Business*. Santa Maria, CA. Puma Publishing Company. 1990.

Antonini, Orlando J. *Getting A Business Loan*, Menlo Park, CA. Crisp Publications. 1993.

Attard, Janet. *The Home Office and Small Business Answer Book*. New York, NY. Henry Holt. 1992.

Bangs, David H. *The Business Planning Guide,* Dover, NH, Upstart Publishing Company. 1992.

Bangs, David H. *The Start-up Guide*. (2nd Edition) Dover, NH. Upstart Publishing Company. 1994.

Bivins, Betty M. *Operating a Really Small Business*. Menlo Park, CA. Crisp Publications. 1994.

Blechman, Bruce Jan and J.C. Levinson. *Guerrilla Financing*. Boston, MA. Houghton Mifflin. 1991.

Christensen, Kathleen. *Women and Home-Based Work*. New York, NY. Henry Holt. 1988.

Clark, Scott A. *Beating the Odds*. New York, NY. AMACOM. 1991.

Clifford, Donald K. and R.E. Cavanagh. *The Winning Performance*. New York, NY. Bantam. 1985.

Cohen, William. *The Entrepreneur and Small Business Problem Solver*. New York, NY. Wiley. 1990.

Covello, Joseph A. and Brian J. Hazelgren. *Your First Business Plan*. Naperville, IL. Source Books Trade. 1993.

Covey, Stephen R. and A.R. and R.R. Merrill. *First Things First*. New York, NY. Simon and Shuster. 1994.

Dickey, Terry. *Budgeting for a Small Business*. Menlo Park, CA. Crisp Publications. 1994.

Dorff, Pat. *File . . . Don't Pile!* New York, NY. St. Martin's Press. 1986.

Eisenberg, Ronni and K. Kelly. *Organize Yourself!* New York, NY. Macmillan. 1988.

Elster, Robert J., *Small Business Sourcebook*. Detroit, MI. Gale Research. 1987.

Fallek, Max. *Finding Money for Your Small Business*. Chicago, IL. Enterprise Dearborn. 1994.

Feingold, S. Norman and Leonard G. Perlman. *Making It On Your Own*. Acropolis Books. 1981.

Fritz, Roger. *Nobody Gets Rich for Somebody Else*. New York, NY. Dodd, Mead & Co. 1981.

Gerson, Richard F. *Marketing Strategies for Small Business*. Menlo Park, CA. Crisp Publications. 1994.

Gibson, Mary Bass. *The Family Circle Book of Careers at Home*. Chicago, IL. Cowles Publishing. 1971.

Gill, James O. *Financial Basics of Small Business Success*. Menlo Park, CA. Crisp Publications. 1994.

Harrison, Lynn. *Extending Credit and Collecting Cash*. Menlo Park, CA. Crisp Publications. 1993.

Huff, Priscilla Y. *101 Best Home-Based Business for Women*. Rocklin, CA. Prima Publishing. 1995.

Kamoroff, Bernard. *Small-Time Operator*. Laytonville, CA. Bell Springs Publishing. 1994.

Katz, Stan J. and A.E. Liu. *Success Trap*. New York, NY. Dell Publishing. 1980.

Kern, Coralee Smith and Tammara Hoffman Wolfram, *How to Run Your Own Home Business*, Lincolnwood, IL, VGM Career Horizons–NTC Publishing Group. 1989.

LeBoeuf, Michael. *Working Smart: How to Accomplish More in Half the Time*. New York, NY. Warner Books. 1979.

Lickson, Charles P. *A Legal Guide for Small Business*. Menlo Park, CA. Crisp Publications. 1995.

Lickson, Charles P. *Ironing It Out: Seven Simple Steps to Resolving Conflict (2d Ed.)*.Menlo Park, CA. Crisp Publications. 1995.

Lickson, Charles P. *Ethics for Government Employees*. Menlo Park, CA. Crisp Publications. 1994.

Lickson, Jeffrey E. *The Continuously Improving Self*. Menlo Park, CA. Crisp Publications. 1992.

Lippitt, Gordon and Ronald. *The Consulting Process in Action*. San Diego, CA. University Associates. 1978.

Magid, Renee Y. and Melissa M. Codkind. *Work and Personal Life*. Menlo Park, CA. Crisp Publications. 1995.

Mancuso, Joseph. *How to Start, Finance and Manage You Own Business*. Englewood Cliffs, NJ. Prentice Hall. 1978.

McKeever, Mike P. *How to Write a Business Plan*. Berkeley, CA. Nolo Press. 1992.

Merrill, Ronald E. *Raising Money*. New York, NY. AMACOM. 1990.

Miller (Lickson), Bryane. *Dignified Departure (2d Ed.)* San Jose, CA. R. & E. Publishers. 1995.

Nicholas, Ted. *Where the Money is and How to Get It*. Wilmington, DE. Enterprise Publishing. 1978.

Northington, Marshall W. *Managing the Family Business*. Menlo Park, CA. Crisp Publications. 1994.

Rubin, Richard. *The Small Business Guide to Borrowing Money*. New York, NY. McGraw-Hill. 1980.

Pollan, Stephen M. and Mark Levine. *The Field Guide to Starting a Business*. New York, NY. Simon and Shuster. 1990.

Trautmann, Carl O. *The Language of Small Business*. Dover, NH. Upstart Publishing Company. 1994.

Williams, Bruce. *In Business for Yourself*. Chelsea, MT. Scarbourgh House. 1991.

Witt, Melanie A. *Job Strategies for People with Disabilities*. Princeton. Peterson's Guide. 1992.

Please note that in addition to the publications listed above, a number of scholarly and lay publications about business frequently contain articles and news about financial strategy issues for the home and small business. Your library's *Readers' Guide to Periodical Literature* is a good place to look for additional material on the subject.

Appendix A.

Preparing Your Home Workspace

In setting up the workspace for your home business, you may find the following checklist helpful in anticipating your home business needs.

    *   A single star beside an entry indicates a one-time purchase.

  **   Two stars indicate the item(s) will have to be replenished.

***   Three stars indicate the item may be produced using your computer and printer.

I. Business

  ☐ Address labels***

  ☐ Briefcase*
    • Hard-sided
    • Expandable

  ☐ Business cards***

  ☐ Computer (portable) case*

  ☐ Credit card(s)**

  ☐ Stationery***
    • Imprinted letterhead
    • Plain second sheets
    • Imprinted envelopes

☐ Note-sized stationery***
  - Imprinted paper
  - Envelopes

II. Calendars

☐ Desk calendar**

☐ Year overview erasable calendar*

☐ "Organizer" notebook*
  - Expense record
  - Refillable extra pages
  - Telephone directory

☐ Portable calendar*

☐ Weekly appointment calendar (to be left in home office)*

III. Communications Center

☐ Stationary telephone with optional services*
  - Call waiting
  - Cancel call waiting
  - Call forwarding
  - Three-way calling
  - Remote call forwarding
  - Call hold
  - Automatic callback
  - Speed calling
  - Voice mail
  - 800 number
  - 900 number

☐ Telephone service with optional extras*
  - Hold button
  - Mute button
  - Automatic redial
  - Number storage
  - Multiline capacity
  - Speaker phone capability

☐ Mobile (cordless) phone within home zone*

☐ Portable (cellular) phone (goes everywhere)*

☐ Fax machine (on separate phone line)*

☐ Pager*

☐ Answering machine*

IV. Computer Equipment

- ☐ Laptop computer (portable)*
- ☐ Stationary computer*
- ☐ Printer*

V. Computer Accessories

- ☐ Disk holders*
- ☐ Disks**
- ☐ Paper**
- ☐ Printer paper**
- ☐ Printer labels**
- ☐ Printer ink**
- ☐ Fireproof safe for storage of important disks*

VI. Office Equipment

- ☐ Bulletin board*
- ☐ Business card holder (either card file or notebook)*
- ☐ Business card file roster (either card file or on computer disk)*
- ☐ Desk*
- ☐ Desk calculator (stationary with tape)*
- ☐ Desk calculator (portable)*
- ☐ Desk chair*
- ☐ Desk clock*
- ☐ Desk lamp*
- ☐ Desk wastebasket*
- ☐ Erasable bulletin board*
- ☐ Desk document/paper shredder*
- ☐ File cabinet(s)*
  - • Stacking plastic crates
  - • Cardboard boxes
- ☐ Hole puncher(s)*

- ☐ Key center*
  - Business vehicle
  - Business office door
  - File cabinets
  - Safe deposit box
  - Strong box
- ☐ Business library center*
  - Books
  - Tapes
  - Videos
- ☐ Library check-out file*
- ☐ Petty cash box*
- ☐ Petty cash voucher file*
- ☐ Photocopier*
  - Stationary
  - Portable
- ☐ Post office box*
  - Large
  - Small
- ☐ Resource file container*
- ☐ Safe deposit box*
- ☐ Strong box*
- ☐ Separate checking account*
- ☐ Separate savings account*
- ☐ Drafting table*
- ☐ Magnifying mirror lamp*
- ☐ Scale meter for mail*
- ☐ Sharpener (electric) for pencils*
- ☐ Stapler*
  - Staple remover
- ☐ Storage*
  - Shelving
  - Warehouse

☐ Stacking trays*

☐ Tape Recorder*
  • Stationary
  • Portable

☐ Tape dispensers*

☐ Television/Video/Video recorder*

☐ Typewriter*

☐ Wall clock*

☐ Working table(s) for packaging/collating*

VII. Office Supplies

☐ Adhesive notepads**

☐ Cellophane tape**

☐ Clear labels**

☐ Clipboards*

☐ Copy paper**

☐ Correction fluid (white plus color to match office supplies)**

☐ Erasers**

☐ Fax paper**

☐ Hanging file folders**
  • Plastic tabs and inserts for file folders

☐ Highlighter markers**

☐ Interior file folders**

☐ Labels for file folders**

☐ Legal pads**

☐ Mailing labels**

☐ Manila envelopes**

☐ Notebooks**
  • 2-ring
  • 3-ring
  • Special binders

☐ Overnight delivery packaging supplies**
  • Federal Express or other private courier

- United States Mail
  - —Express
  - —Overnight
  - —Registered
- ☐ Paper clips**
- ☐ Pencils**
- ☐ Pens**
- ☐ Postage stamps**
- ☐ Postal meter*
- ☐ Printing ink pad for various stamps**
- ☐ Rubber bands**
- ☐ Rulers*
- ☐ Stamps**
  - Check endorsement stamp
    - —Checking account
    - —Savings account
  - Date stamp
  - Employee name/title stamp
  - Postage stamp
  - Priority mail stamp
    - —Critical
    - —High priority
    - —Immediate
    - —Rush
  - "Sensitivity" stamps
    - —Company confidential
    - —Highly sensitive information
    - —Trade secret information
- ☐ Staples**

VIII. Business Coverage Documents

- ☐ Insurance Policies**
  - Equipment
  - Facility
  - Personal
  - Disaster
- ☐ Licenses**

☐ Permits**

☐ Resale tax number*

☐ Tax ID number*

☐ Tax-exemption number*

IX. Employees

☐ Special Employee
  - Job title/salary or independent contractor

☐ General Employee
  - Number of full-time or part-time
  - Job title
  - Wages and benefits

☐ Total estimated wages to be paid
  - Weekly
  - Monthly
  - Quarterly
  - Yearly

APPENDIX B.
Sample Forms

Certificate of Doing Business

TOWN CLERK'S OFFICE
CENTRAL CITY, VA 22000

Please take notice that David Reuban of Central City is conducting an un-incorporated business known as "David Reuban Associates" located at 101 Apple Avenue, Central City, VA 22000.

Dated at Central City, this _____ day of _____ , 1996.

_____

David Reuban

Local business License No: _____

Note: These forms will vary from jurisdiction to jurisdiction. Check with your city, town or county clerk or clerk of court to see how you go about obtaining a local certificate to do business and business license if required by law.

Simple Partnership Agreement

AGREEMENT made as of this 14th day of February, 1996, between David Reuban of Central City, VA ("Reuban") and Mary Jones of Middleburg, VA ("Jones").

The parties intend to form a partnership to conduct a management consulting and business advisory firm on the following terms and conditions:

1. The partnership shall become effective upon the signing of this agreement and the paying in of $6,000 contribution by Reuban and $4,000 by Jones.

2. The partnership shall be known as David Reuban Associates.

3. The partnership will engage in the business of a full-service management consulting and business advisory service.

4. Business location will be 101 Apple Avenue, Central City, VA 00011.

5. The partnership shall continue so long as both partners shall be alive. It may terminate sooner by agreement of the parties.

6. Profits and losses in the partnership shall be allocated 60% to Reuban and 40% to Jones.

7. Partners shall draw a sum to be mutually agreed upon but not less than $200 per week.

8. Both partners shall devote full time and attention to the business of the partnership.

9. Reuban shall be designated as the Managing Partner and shall have responsibility for the business and financial affairs of the partnership. Jones shall be designated as the Development Partner and have primary responsibility for creative efforts and marketing for the partnership.

10. At the dissolution of the partnership for any reason, the surplus, if any, shall be distributed 60% to Reuban and 40% to Jones. The name and goodwill, if any, shall be sold with proceeds to be divided equally.

11. In the event of disagreement under this agreement or in running the affairs of the partnership, the partners agree to submit all unresolved issues to mediation prior to taking any legal action.

12. This agreement is the whole agreement of the parties with respect to the subject matter; it may not be amended except in writing; it may not be assigned by either party; and it shall be governed by the Laws of the Commonwealth of Virginia.

Signed at Central City, VA.

_____

David Reuban

_____

Mary Jones

AFFIDAVIT

City of Central City   }

                              }   ss: Virginia

County of Windsor   }

On this 14th day of February 1996, came David Reuban and Mary Jones who each identified themselves to me and swore before me that their signatures on the foregoing document were their free act and deed.

_____

I. M. Onnest
Notary Public No. 1009
(My commission expires 12-23-97)

ARTICLES OF INCORPORATION

OF

DAMYN COMPANY, INC.

The undersigned, pursuant to Chapter 9 of Title 13.1 of the Code of Virginia, hereby executes the following articles of incorporation and sets forth the following:

1. The name of the corporation is: Damyn Company, Inc.

2. The nature of the business and purposes to be transacted, promoted and carried on: are to engage in any lawful act or activity for which corporations may be organized under the General Corporation Laws of Virginia.

3. The total amount of the total authorized capital stock of this corporation is five thousand (5,000) shares of common stock of one cent ($.01) par value.

4. The post office address of the initial registered office is:

   101 Apple Avenue
   Central City, VA 22000

   and the name of the initial registered agent at such address is David Reuban who is a resident of Virginia and an officer and director of the corporation.

5. The names and addresses of the directors are:

David Reuban	101 Apple Avenue Central City, VA 22000
Mary Jones	10 Horseplay Lane Middleburg, VA 22000
Phyllis Reuban	101 Apple Avenue Central City, VA 22000

6. The registered office is located in the City of Central City.

INCORPORATOR:

_____

David Reuban
Date: April 25, 1996

Note: *Most states have a printed form for simple corporations. These forms are available from the State Corporation Commission, Secretary of State or other agency administering corporations.*

Appendix C

Outline of a Comprehensive Business Plan
(With Three-Year Projections)

☐ Cover Sheet: Name of business, names of principals, address and phone number

☐ Statement of Purpose of the Firm

☐ Table of Contents

☐ Executive Summary

☐ Section One: The Business
- Description of Business
- Product Service
- The Market
- Location of Business
- Competition
- Management/Personnel
- Application and Expected Effect of Capital
- Summary

☐ Section Two: Financial Data
- Sources and Applications of Funding
- Capital Equipment List (If Any)
- Balance Sheet
- Break-Even Analysis

Covello, and Hazelgren. *Your First Business Plan.* Naperville, Illinois: Trade Source Books. 1993.

- Income Projections (Profit and Loss Statements)
  - —Three-year summary
  - —Detail by month for first year
  - —Detail by quarter for second and third years
  - —Notes (of explanation)
- Cash Flow Projection
  - —Detail by month for first year
  - —Detail by quarter for second and third years
  - —Notes (of explanation)
- Deviation Analysis (Optional)
- Historical Financial Reports (for Existing Business Only)
  - —Balance sheets for past three years
  - —Income statements for past three years
  - —Tax returns

☐ Section Three: Supporting Documents

Personal résumés, personal balance sheets, cost-of-living budget, credit reports, letters of reference, job descriptions, letters of intent, copies of real estate and equipment leases, significant contracts, legal documents, other materials relevant to the plan.

NOTES

NOTES

NOTES

NOTES